Basic Bookkeeping

For the 2003 Standards

August 2003

Interactive Text

In this August 2003 first edition

- Material rewritten for the new standards
- Layout designed to be easier on the eye – and easy to use
- Clear language and presentation

BPP
PROFESSIONAL EDUCATION

First edition August 2003

ISBN 0 7517 1227 2

British Library Cataloguing-in-Publication Data
A catalogue record for this book
is available from the British Library

Published by

BPP Professional Education
Aldine House, Aldine Place
London W12 8AW

www.bpp.com

Printed in Great Britain by W M Print
45-47 Frederick Street
Walsall, West Midlands
WS2 9NE

Contents

Page

Order form

Review form & free prize draw

iii

chapter 1

Double entry bookkeeping

Contents

1 The problem

We need a way of transferring information about business transactions into the books of account.

Any method of writing up the books (bookkeeping), needs to satisfy the following.

- Reflect the commercial reality of the transaction
- Be recorded accurately
- Any errors can be spotted relatively easily

2 The solution

The solution is called **double entry bookkeeping**.

Double entry bookkeeping was invented to help medieval Italian bankers keep records of the people who gave them money to invest and those who borrowed from them.

The bankers realised that each transaction had a **two-fold** effect on the business.

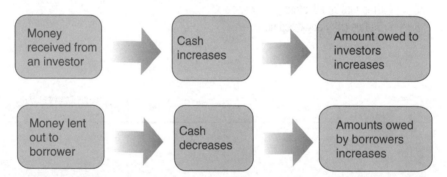

Double entry bookkeeping reflects this two-fold effect by requiring two entries in the books for every transaction.

The two entries are called **debits** and **credits**. For every debit entry, there must be an equal credit entry. So when all transactions have been entered:

If total debits do not equal total credits, then an error has been made.

3 Business basics

Before looking at the mechanics of double entry, what do we mean by a **business**?

- A business manufactures, sells or supplies **goods and services**.

- A business uses **economic resources** to create goods or services which customers will buy.

- A business is an organisation **providing jobs** for people to work in.

- A business invests money to make even **more money for its owners.**

This last definition – investing money to make money – introduces the key idea of **profit**.

Businesses vary in character, size and complexity. They range from small businesses (the local shopkeeper or plumber) to very large ones (ICI or BP).

However they all want to **earn a profit**.

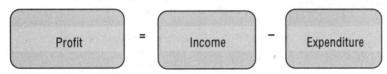

If expenditure exceeds income, then a **loss** is made.

Double entry bookkeeping records income and expenditure in order to be able to calculate profit.

However, double entry bookkeeping goes further than this, it also records what a business **owns** (assets) and what it **owes** (liabilities)

4 Assets and liabilities

4.1 Assets

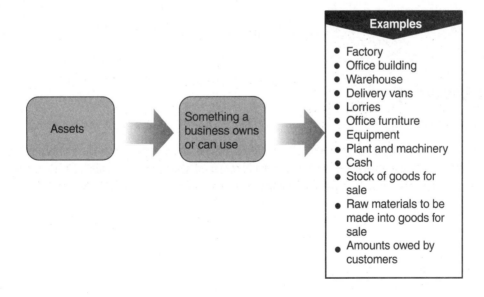

4.2 Fixed assets

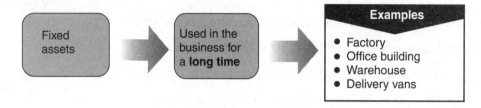

4.3 Current assets

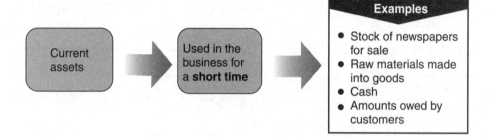

4.4 Liabilities

4.5 Capital

Examples: Ownership

(a)   Limited company

A limited company is owned by its shareholders. In **law**, the company is separate from the shareholders. The company can make contracts in its own name, hold assets and owe liabilities. The shareholders are not responsible for the company's liabilities. The shareholders' liability is **limited** to the amount they pay for their shares.

(b)   **Partnership**

A partnership is owned by two or more people. A, B and C may trade as ABC Building Supplies. However, because ABC Building Supplies is not a limited company, A, B and C are legally responsible for all the amounts owed by the partnership.

(c)   **Sole trader**

A sole trader, Sonia, may trade as Sonia's Hair Salon. However, legally Sonia and her hair salon are one and the same.

In the above examples, **the law** sees no difference between a business run by a sole trader or partnership and the owner(s).

However, for **accounts purposes**, the business is always treated as a separate **entity** from its owners.

So when an owner puts money into a business, for accounts purposes this is treated as a liability of the business, and it is called **capital.**

Activity 1.1

Complete the grid below, by ticking the appropriate column for each item.

	Asset	Liability	Capital
Bank overdraft			
Factory			
Money paid into a business by the owner			
Bank account			
Plant and machinery			
Amounts due from customers			
Amounts due from suppliers			
Stock of goods for sale			

5 The accounting equation

The **accounting equation** states that the **assets** and **liabilities** of a business must always be **equal.**

Assets	=	Liabilities

However, as we saw in Section 4.5 above, **capital** is a form of liability, so we can restate the accounting equation.

Assets	=	Liabilities	+	Capital

Example: Accounting equation

On 1 July 20X7, Petula opens a market stall selling perfume. She puts £2,500 from her savings into the business. From an accountant's viewpoint, the business has cash of £2,500 but owes Petula capital of £2,500.

Assets	=	Liabilities	+	Capital
Cash £2,500	=	£0	+	£2,500

As a business trades, there will be changes in the assets and liabilities. However, the accounting equation will always apply.

Example: Trading and profit

On 2 July 20X7, Petula buys 100 bottles of perfume for £1,000 and sells all of them on her market stall for £1,500 cash. How do these transactions affect the accounting equation?

(a) **Purchase of perfume**

	Assets	=	Liabilities	+	Capital
Perfume	£1,000				
Cash	£1,500				
(2,500 – 1,000)					
	£2,500		£0		£2,500

(b) **Sale of perfume**

Petula has sold all her perfume for £1,500 but it only cost her £1,000. Remember profit = income – expenditure.

Profit = 1,500 – 1,000
= £500

Profit is earned by the business, but how is this reflected in the accounts? Profit is owed to the owner of the business and so is **added to capital.**

	Assets	=	Liabilities	+	Capital	
Perfume (1,000 – 1,000)	£0				Capital	£2,500
Cash	£3,000				Profit	£500
(1,500 + 1,500)					(1,500 – 1,000)	
	£3,000		£0			£3,000

So far we have only considered cash transactions. What happens to the accounting equation if credit transactions occur?

Also what happens if an owner takes money out of the business? For accounting purposes, the money an owner takes out of a business is called **drawings.**

Example: Credit and drawings

On 3 July 20X7, Petula buys 200 bottles of perfume for £2,000. However she agrees with the supplier that she will pay for the perfume in 7 days' time.

In the market that day Petula sells all the perfume for £3,000. She then takes out £500 for her personal use.

(a)   **Purchase of perfume on credit**

	Assets	=	Liabilities		+	Capital	
Perfume	£2,000	Owed to supplier	£2,000			Capital b/f	£3,000
Cash	£3,000						
	£5,000		£2,000				£3,000

(b)   **Sales of perfume**

Petula has sold all her perfume

$$Profit = income - expenditure$$
$$= 3,000 - 2,000$$
$$= £1,000$$

	Assets	=	Liabilities		+	Capital	
Perfume	£0	Owed to supplier	£2,000			Capital b/f	£3,000
(2,000 – 2,000)							
Cash	£6,000					Profit	£1,000
(3,000 + 3,000)						(3,000 – 2,000)	
	£6,000		£2,000				£4,000

(c)   **Drawings**

	Assets	=	Liabilities		+	Capital	
Perfume	£0	Owed to supplier	£2,000			Capital b/f	£3,000
Cash	£5,500					Profit	£1,000
(6,000 – 500)						Drawings	£(500)
	£5,500		£2,000				£3,500

From the above examples, we can see

Capital	=	Capital introduced	+	Profit	−	Drawings

Activity 1.2

Joanne has purchased goods totalling £25,000. She paid cash of £10,000 and the rest has been bought on credit. She has only just started trading and put £20,000 cash into the business from her savings. Use the grid below to calculate the accounting equation.

Assets = *Liabilities* + *Capital*

Activity 1.3

Joanne has sold all her goods for £50,000. She withdraws £5,000 for her own use. Using the information from Activity 1.2 above, complete the grid below.

Assets = *Liabilities* + *Capital*

BPP
PROFESSIONAL EDUCATION

6 The business equation

As we saw above:

Assets	=	Liabilities	+	Capital

Also

Capital	=	Capital introduced	+	Profit	−	Drawings

So the accounting equation can be restated as:

Assets	=	Liabilities	+	Capital introduced	+	Profit	−	Drawings

If you think about it, capital can be introduced in any period. Also profit is earned in different periods.

Assets	=	Liabilities	+	Capital introduced in current period	+	Capital introduced in previous periods	+	Profit earned in current period	+	Profit earned in previous periods	−	Drawings

The **business equation** is a way of calculating the profit earned in a period.

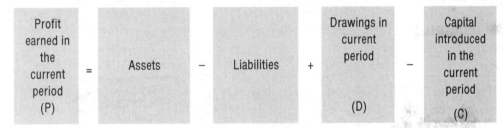

Profit earned in the current period (P)	=	Assets	−	Liabilities	+	Drawings in current period (D)	−	Capital introduced in the current period (C)

Assets less liabilities are also known as **net assets.** So if I is the increase in net assets in the current period: P = I + D − C

Activity 1.4

Joanne has now been in business for a year. At the beginning she introduced capital of £20,000. At the end of the year, her net assets were £50,000 and her drawings totalled £5,000. What was her profit for the year? Use the grid below.

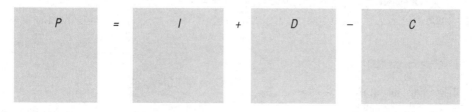

| P | = | I | + | D | – | C |

7 Creditors and debtors

What happens when we make sales on credit and purchases on credit?

7.1 Sale on credit

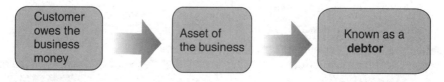

Customer owes the business money → Asset of the business → Known as a **debtor**

7.2 Purchase on credit

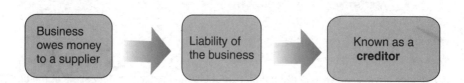

Business owes money to a supplier → Liability of the business → Known as a **creditor**

Activity 1.5

(a)   Joanne buys good totalling £75,000. She pays cash of £15,000. How much does she owe her creditors?

(b)   Joanne has sold goods totalling £150,000. If £50,000 of this was a cash sale, how much is owed by her debtors?

8 Double entry book-keeping

We are now in a position to look at the bookkeeping entries of the business.

8.1 Recap

In Section 2, we looked at the two-fold nature of a business transaction and, in Section 5, we looked at that two-fold action in practice.

A **debit** is used to record increases in **assets.**

A **credit** is used to record increases in **liabilities** or **capital**

From Section 5, the accounting equation states:

So from the two-fold nature of transactions:

| Total debits | = | Total credits |

8.2 Double-entry bookkeeping

Transactions are usually recorded in a 'T' account, with debits on the left hand side and credits on the right.

ACCOUNT NAME	
DEBITS	CREDITS

The two sides of the 'T' represent the two sides of the accounting equation.

ACCOUNT	
DEBITS	CREDITS
Assets	**Liabilities**
	Capital

So a debit will **increase** an asset and a credit will **decrease** an asset. Similarly a credit will **increase** a liability and a debit will decrease it.

ANY ASSET ACCOUNT		ANY LIABILITY ACCOUNT		CAPITAL ACCOUNT	
Increase	Decrease	Decrease	Increase	Decrease	Increase

Remember that:

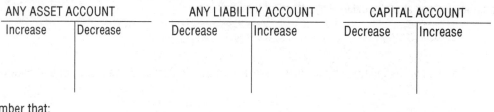

Capital = Capital introduced + Profit − Drawings

As profit increases capital, profit will be a **credit** entry in the accounts. However drawings decrease capital and so drawings will be a **debit** entry.

Profit can be stated as:

Profit = Income − Expenditure

Income increases profit and so is a **credit** entry, while expenditure decreases profit and so is a **debit** entry.

8.3 Summary

DEBIT	CREDIT
Assets	**Capital**
Expenditure	**Liabilities**
	Income

ASSET		LIABILITY		CAPITAL	
Debit	**Credit**	**Debit**	**Credit**	**Debit**	**Credit**
Increase	Decrease	Decrease	Increase	Decrease	Increase

INCOME		EXPENDITURE	
Debit	**Credit**	**Debit**	**Credit**
Decrease	Increase	Increase	Decrease

PROFESSIONAL EDUCATION

8.4 Accounting for VAT

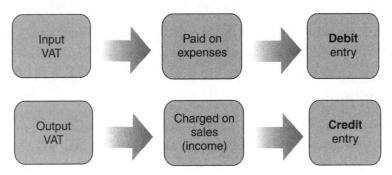

Therefore the VAT account is

VAT

Debit	Credit
Input VAT	Output VAT

Example: Double entry

Consider the position of Petula at the end of 3 July 20X7. What transactions have been carried out since she started business on 1 July 20X7 and what is the double entry?

(a)   **1 July 20X7**

		Debit	Credit
(i)	Introduction of cash – increases asset of cash and increases capital owed to Petula	Cash: £2,500	Capital: £2,500

(b)   **2 July 20X7**

		Debit	Credit
(i)	Purchase of perfume – increases expense of purchases for sale and decreases asset of cash	Purchases: £1,000	Cash: £1,000
(ii)	Sale of perfume – cash increased by £1,500, sales income increased by £1,500	Cash: £1,500	Sales: £1,500

(c)   **3 July 20X7**

		Debit	Credit
(i)	**Purchase on credit** Purchases of perfumes increased and creditors increased	Purchases: £2,000	Creditors: £2,000
(ii)	**Sale of perfume** Cash increased by £3,000 and sales income increased by £3,000	Cash: £3,000	Sales: £3,000

(iii) **Drawings**

Cash decreased and drawings increased   Drawings: £500   Cash: £500

Tutorial note. In practice, purchases of stock are posted to a purchases account and sales to a sales account. It is only at the end of the period of account that the profit or loss is calculated by deducting expenses (including purchases) from income (sales). This is because it is not practical to calculate the profit or loss arising on each transaction.

Example: Entries in the accounts

If we post the entries to the 'T' accounts, we get the following position.

CASH

		£			£
1.7.X7	Capital	2,500	2.7.X7	Purchases	1,000
2.7.X7	Sales	1,500	3.7.X7	Drawings (capital)	500
3.7.X7	Sales	3,000			

CAPITAL

		£			£
3.7.X7	Cash	500	1.7.X7	Cash	2,500

PURCHASES

		£		£
2.7.X7	Cash	1,000		
3.7.X7	Creditors	2,000		

SALES

	£			£
		2.7.X7	Cash	1,500
		3.7.X7	Cash	3,000

CREDITORS

	£			£
		3.7.X7	Purchases	2,000

Notice that the narrative shows where the other half of the double entry can be found.

Activity 1.6

Complete the grid below to reflect the double entry for the following transactions.

Debit   *Credit*

(a)   Loan of £5,000 received from the bank

(b)   A payment of £800 cash for purchases

(c)   The owner takes £50 cash to buy a birthday present for her husband

(d)   The business sells goods costing £300 for £450 cash

(e)   The business sells goods costing £300 for £450 on credit

Key learning points

☑ It is vital that you acquire a thorough understanding of the **principles of double entry bookkeeping**.

☑ A **business** may be defined in various ways. Its purpose is to make a **profit** for its owner(s).

☑ **Profit** is the excess of income over expenditure.

☑ A business **owns assets** and **owes liabilities**.

☑ For accounting purposes it is important to keep business assets and liabilities **separate** from the personal assets and liabilities of the owners.

☑ **Assets** are items belonging to a business and used in the running of the business. They may be **fixed** (such as machinery or office premises), or **current** (such as stock, debtors and cash).

☑ **Liabilities** are sums of money owed by a business to outsiders such as a bank or a trade creditor.

☑ **Assets = Capital + Liabilities** (the accounting equation).

☑ **P = I + D − C** (the business equation).

☑ Double entry book-keeping requires that every transaction has two accounting entries, a **debit** and a **credit**.

☑ After all transactions have been posted, **total debits must equal total credits**.

Quick quiz

1 What is a business's prime objective?

2 Define profit.

3 Which of the following is an asset?

   A Bank overdraft
   B Creditors
   C Debtors
   D Capital

4 Which of the following is a liability?

   A Factory
   B Stock
   C Bank overdraft
   D Debtors

5 How does the accounting view of the relationship between a business and its owner differ from the strictly legal view?

6 State the basic accounting equation.

7 What is capital?

8 What are drawings? Where do they fit in the accounting equation?

9 What does the business equation attempt to show?

10 What is the main difference between a cash and a credit transaction?

11 What is a creditor? What is a debtor?

12 Define double entry bookkeeping.

13 What is the double entry for a credit purchase?

Answers to quick quiz

1   A business's prime objective is earning a profit.

2   Profit is the excess of income over expenditure.

3   C Debtors

4   C Bank overdraft

5   In accounting a business is always treated as a separate entity from its owners, even though in law there is not always a distinction (in the cases of a sole trader and a partnership).

6   Assets = Capital + Liabilities.

7   Capital is the investment of funds with the intention of earning a profit.

8   Drawings are the amounts of money taken out of a business by its owner. In the accounting equation drawings are a reduction of capital.

9   The business equation describes the relationship between a business's increase in net assets in a period, the profit earned, drawings taken and capital introduced.

10   The main difference between a cash and a credit transaction is simply a matter of time – cash changes hands immediately in a cash transaction, whereas in a credit one it changes hands some time after the initial sale/purchase takes place.

11   A creditor is a person that a business owes money to, while a debtor is a person who owes a business money.

12   Double entry bookkeeping is a system of accounting which reflects the fact that every financial transaction gives rise to two equal accounting entries, a debit and a credit.

13   DEBIT   Purchases
     CREDIT   Creditors

chapter 2

Recording, summarising and posting transactions

Contents

1 The problem

In the last chapter, we looked at double entry bookkeeping. However how do we use double entry to record transactions?

There are a vast number of transactions every day in large businesses. It takes a lot of time to enter every individual transactions in the accounts. Is there a short cut?

2 The solution

The individual invoices, credit notes and cheques (called **source documents**) are recorded in **day books**. The **totals** of the day books are then **posted** into the accounts using double entry bookkeeping.

In summary:

3 Recording business transactions: an overview

3.1 Source documents

Source documents are the source of all the information recorded by a business.

Source documents include the following.

- Invoices
- Credit notes
- Petty cash vouchers
- Cheques received
- Cheque stubs (for cheques paid out)
- Wages, salaries and PAYE records

3.2 Why do we need to record source documents?

During the course of its trade, a business sends out and receives *many* source documents. The details on these source documents need to be recorded, otherwise the business might forget to ask for some money, or forget to pay some, or even accidentally pay something twice. In other words, it needs to **keep records of source documents** – of transactions – so that it can keep tabs on what is going on.

3.3 How do we record them?

In **books of prime entry**.

Books of prime entry form the record of all the documents sent out and received by the business.

Book of prime entry	Documents recorded	Summarised and posted to
Sales day book/Sales returns day book	Sales invoices, credit notes sent	Sales ledger/control account in main ledger
Purchase day book/Purchase returns day book	Purchase invoices, credit notes received	Purchase ledger/control account in main ledger
Cash book	Cash paid and received	Main ledger
Petty cash book	Notes and coin paid and received	Main ledger
Journal	Adjustments	Main ledger

Activity 2.1

State which books of prime entry the following transactions would be entered into.

(a)   Your business pays A Brown (a supplier) £450.
(b)   You send D Steptoe (a customer) an invoice for £650.
(c)   You receive an invoice from A Brown for £300.
(d)   You pay D Steptoe £500.
(e)   F Jones (a customer) returns goods to the value of £250.
(f)   You return goods to J Green to the value of £504.
(g)   F Jones pays you £500.

TERMINOLOGY ALERT

The AAT uses specific terminology.

Main ledger – this is the same as **general or nominal ledger**.

Subsidiary ledger – this is the same as:

*   **Sales (debtors) ledger AND**
*   **Purchases (creditors) ledger**

In this text we will use sales and purchases ledger rather than subsidiary ledger because you need to tell them apart.

3.4 Summarising source documents

Due to the large number of source documents, and that they come from and are sent to a very large number of suppliers and customers, it is vital that the information in them is **summarised.** This is done in two ways.

Ledger used	Need for summary
Subsidiary ledgers Sales ledger Purchase ledger	Summaries need to be kept of all the transactions undertaken with an individual supplier or customer – invoices, credit notes, cash – so that a net amount due or owed can be calculated.
Main ledger (a) Sales ledger control account (b) Purchase ledger control account	Summaries need to be kept of all the transactions undertaken with all suppliers and customers, so a total for debtors and a total for creditors can be calculated.

We will look at the subsidiary ledger and control accounts in more detail later in this Text.

3.5 Posting the ledgers

Have a look at the diagram on the next page. It shows how items are **posted** to (**entered in**) the ledgers, ultimately to arrive at the financial statements. Don't worry that some of the terms are unfamiliar at the moment – you will understand it all when you have completed this Text.

4 The sales day book

The **sales day book** is a list of all invoices sent out to **customers** each day.

4.1 Using the sales day book

An extract from a sales day book, ignoring VAT for the moment, might look like this.

SALES DAY BOOK

Date 20X7	Invoice number (2)	Customer	Sales ledger folio (1)	Total amount invoiced £
Jan 10	247	James Ltd	SL14	105.00
	248	Steptoe & Son	SL 8	86.40
	249	Talbot & Co	SL 6	31.80
	250	John Silvertown	SL 9	1,264.60
				1,487.80

(1)   The 'sales ledger folio' refers to a page (called a folio) for the individual customer in the **sales ledger**. It means, for example, that the sale to James Ltd for £105 is also recorded on page 14 of the sales ledger.

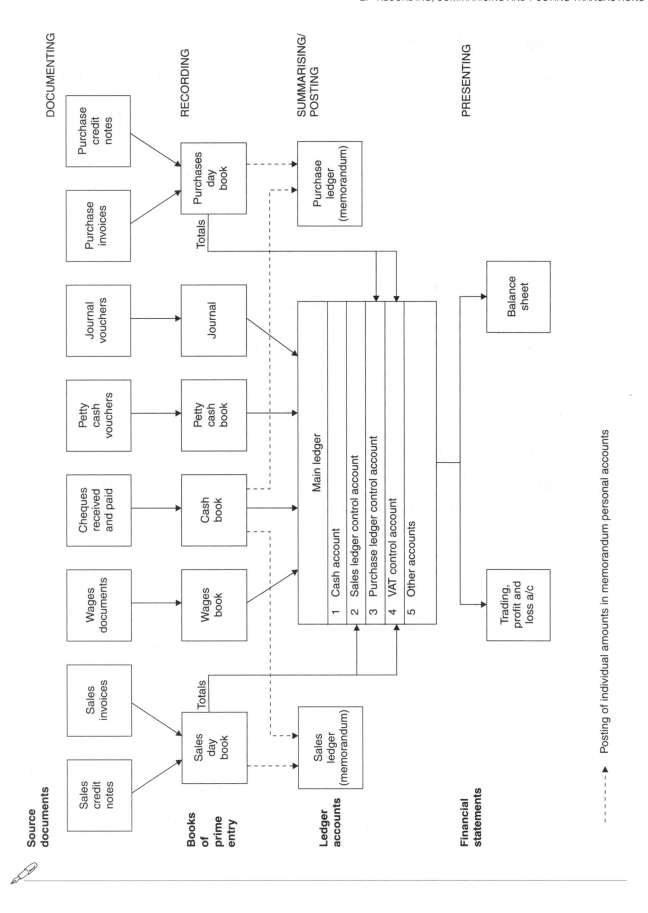

(2)   The invoice number is the **unique number** given to each sales invoice by the business's sales system. Listing them out sequentially in the sales day book helps us to see that all the invoices are included.

4.2 Sales analysis

Most businesses 'analyse' their sales. For example, suppose that the business sells boots and shoes, and that the sale to Steptoe was entirely boots, the sale to Talbot was entirely shoes, and the other two sales were a mixture of both.

Then the sales day book might look like this.

SALES DAY BOOK

Date 20X7	Invoice	Customer	Sales ledger folio	Total amount invoiced £	Boot sales £	Shoe sales £
Jan 10	247	James Ltd	SL 14	105.00	60.00	45.00
	248	Steptoe & Son	SL 8	86.40	86.40	
	249	Talbot & Co	SL 6	31.80		31.80
	250	John Silvertown	SL 9	1,264.60	800.30	464.30
				1,487.80	946.70	541.10

This sort of analysis gives the managers of the business useful information which helps them to decide how best to run the business.

4.3 The sales returns day book

When customers return goods for some reason, the returns are recorded in the **sales returns day book**.

An extract from the sales returns day book might look like this.

SALES RETURNS DAY BOOK

Date 20X7	Customer and goods	Sales ledger folio	Amount £
30 April	Owen Plenty		
	3 pairs 'Texas' boots	SL 82	135.00

Not all sales returns day books analyse what goods were returned, but it makes sense to keep as complete a record as possible.

Sales returns could alternatively be shown as **bracketed figures in the sales day book.** This usually happens in a business that very rarely has sales returns.

5 The purchase day book

The **purchase day book** is the record of all the invoices received from **suppliers.**

5.1 Using the purchase day book

An extract from a purchase day book might look like this ignoring VAT.

PURCHASE DAY BOOK

Date	Supplier (2)	Purchase ledger folio (1)	Total amount invoiced	Purchases (3)	Expenses
20X7			£	£	£
Mar 15	Sugar & Spice	PL 31	315.00	315.00	
	F Seager	PL 46	29.40	29.40	
	ABC	PL 42	116.80		116.80
	Shabnum Rashid	PL 12	100.00	100.00	
			561.20	444.40	116.80

(1)   The 'purchase ledger folio' refers to a page for the individual supplier in the purchase ledger.

(2)   There is no 'invoice number' column, because the purchase day book records **other people's invoices**, which have all sorts of different numbers. Sometimes a purchase day book may use an internal number for an invoice.

(3)   Like the sales day book, the purchase day book analyses the invoices which have been sent in. In this example, three of the invoices related to goods for resale ('purchases') and the fourth invoice was an electricity bill.

5.2 The purchase returns day book

The **purchase returns day book** is kept to record credit notes received in respect of goods which the business sends back to its suppliers.

The business expects a **credit note** from the supplier. In the meantime, it might issue a **debit note** to the supplier, indicating the amount by which the business expects its total debt to the supplier to be reduced.

An extract from the purchase returns day book might look like this.

PURCHASE RETURNS DAY BOOK

Date	Supplier and goods	Purchase ledger folio	Amount
20X7			£
29 April	Boxes Ltd		
	300 cardboard boxes	PL 123	46.60

Purchase returns could be shown as **bracketed figures** in the purchase day book.

6 The cash book

The **cash book** is a book of prime entry, used to keep a cumulative record of money received and money paid out by the business **via its bank account**.

Money received includes receipts **on the business premises** in notes, coins and cheques which are subsequently banked. There are also receipts and payments made by bank transfer, standing order, direct debit, BACS and, in the case of bank interest and charges, directly by the bank.

6.1 Using the cash book

One part of the cash book is used to record **receipts of cash**, and another part is used to **record payments**. Below is a summary of what a cash book looks like

		LEFT HAND SIDE: RECEIPTS					RIGHT HAND SIDE: PAYMENTS		
Date	Narrative	Discount allowed	Receipt	Analysis	Date	Narrative	Discount received	Payment	Analysis
		£10	£100	£100			£7	£90	£90

Note the following points about this cash book.

(a)   It represents two sides of a **ledger account**: the left hand receipts side is DEBIT, the right hand payments side is CREDIT (see Section 7 below).

(b)   It is a **two-column cash book** – on the debit side there are two columns: one column for total receipts and one for discounts allowed; on the credit side there are also two columns – one for total payments and one for discounts received.

(c)   Discounts allowed (given) and received are **memorandum columns** only – they do not represent cash movements.

(d)   On each side, the 'analysis' can be one or more columns; **the total of the analysis columns *always* equals the total receipts or total payments.**

The best way to see how the cash book works is to follow through an example. **Note that in this example we are continuing to ignore VAT.**

Example: Cash book

At the beginning of 1 September, Liz Cullis had £900 in the bank. During 1 September 20X7, Liz Cullis had the following receipts and payments.

(a)   Cash sale: receipt of £80
(b)   Payment from credit customer Hay: £400 less discount allowed £20
(c)   Payment from credit customer Been: £720
(d)   Payment from credit customer Seed: £1,000 less discount allowed £40
(e)   Cash sale: receipt of £150
(f)   Cash received for sale of machine: £200

(g)   Payment to supplier Kew: £120
(h)   Payment to supplier Hare: £310
(i)   Payment of telephone bill: £400
(j)   Payment of gas bill: £280
(k)   Payment of £1,500 to Hess for new plant and machinery

If you look through these transactions, you will see that six of them are receipts and five of them are payments.

Solution

The cash book for Liz Cullis is shown on the following page.

In a standard two-column cash book:

- Receipts and payments are listed out on either side of the cash book – **receipts** on the **left** (increase **asset** = debit) and **payments** on the **right** (decrease **asset** = credit).

- Both sides have columns for these details.

    – Date
    – Narrative
    – Folio reference
    – **Total**
    – **Discount allowed/received**

- Each side has a number of **columns for further analysis** – receipts from debtors, cash sales and other receipts; payments to creditors, expenses and fixed assets.

6.2 Balancing the cash book

At the beginning of the day there is a debit **opening balance** of £900 on Liz Cullis's cash book. During the day, the total receipts and payments were as follows.

	£
Opening balance	900
Receipts	2,490
	3,390
Payments	(2,610)
Closing balance	780

The **closing balance** of £780 represents the excess of receipts over payments. It means that Liz Cullis still has cash available at the end of the day, so she 'carries it down' at the end of 1 September from the payments side of the cash book, and 'brings it down' at the beginning of 2 September to the receipts side of the cash book.

Balance b/d	Balance brought down	Opening balance
Balance c/d	Balance carried down	Closing balance
Balance b/f	Balance brought forward	Opening balance
Balance c/f	Balance carried forward	Closing balance

LIZ CULLIS: CASH BOOK

RECEIPTS

Date 20X7	Narrative	Folio	Discount allowed £	Total £	Receipts from debtors £	Cash sales £	Other £
01-Sep	Balance b/d (= opening bal)			900			
	(a) Cash sale			80		80	
	(b) Debtor pays: Hay	SL96	20	380	380		
	(c) Debtor pays: Been	SL632		720	720		
	(d) Debtor pays: Seed	SL501	40	960	960		
	(e) Cash sale			150		150	
	(f) Fixed asset sale			200			200
			60	3,390	2,060	230	200
02-Sep	Balance b/d (= new opening bal)			780			

PAYMENTS

Date 20X7	Narrative	Folio	Total £	Payments to creditors	Expenses	Fixed assets
01-Sep	(g) Creditor paid: Kew	PL543	120	120		
	(h) Creditor paid: Hare	PL76	310	310		
	(i) Telephone expense		400		400	
	(j) Gas expense		280		280	
	(k) Plant & machinery		1,500			1,500
			2,610	430	680	1,500
	Balance c/d (= closing bal)		780			
			3,390	430	680	1,500

6.3 Bank statements

Weekly or monthly, a business will receive a **bank statement**. Bank statements should be used to check that the amount shown as a balance in the cash book agrees with the amount on the bank statement, and that no cash has 'gone missing'. This is called a **bank reconciliation** (see Chapter 8).

6.4 Petty cash book

The **petty cash book** is the book of prime entry which keeps a cumulative record of the small amounts of cash received into and paid out of the cash float.

This is for small items. For example, your business may keep a 'float' of £50 to pay milk bills, reimburse staff travel costs etc.

7 The main ledger

The **main ledger** is the accounting record which summarises the financial affairs of a business. It contains details of assets, liabilities and capital, income and expenditure, and so profit and loss.

It consists of a large number of different **ledger accounts**, each account having its own purpose or 'name' and an identity or code.

Other names for the main ledger are the **nominal ledger** or **general ledger**.

Transactions are **posted** to accounts in the main ledger from the books of prime entry.

Often posting is done in total (ie all sales invoices in the sales day book for a day are added up and the total is posted to the sales ledger control account) but individual transactions are also posted (eg fixed assets).

Here are some examples of ledger accounts in the main ledger.

Ledger account	Fixed asset	Current asset	Current liability	Long-term liability	Capital	Expense	Income
Plant and machinery at cost	✓						
Motor vehicles at cost	✓						
Proprietor's capital					✓		
Purchases of raw materials						✓	
Stock of raw materials		✓					
Sales ledger control		✓					
Purchase ledger control			✓				
Wages and salaries						✓	
Rent						✓	
Advertising expenses						✓	

Ledger account	Fixed asset	Current asset	Current liability	Long-term liability	Capital	Expense	Income
Bank charges						✓	
Motor expenses						✓	
Telephone expenses						✓	
Sales							✓
Cash		✓					
Bank overdraft			✓				
Bank loan				✓			

7.1 The format of a ledger account

If a ledger account were to be kept in an actual book rather than as a computer record, its **format** might be as follows.

ADVERTISING EXPENSES

Date	Narrative	Folio	£	Date	Narrative	Folio	£
20X7							
15 April	AbFab Agency for quarter to 31 March	PL 348	2,500				

There are two sides to the account, and an account heading on top, and so it is often called a 'T' account.

NAME OF ACCOUNT

DEBIT SIDE (DR)	£	CREDIT SIDE (CR)	£

We have already seen this with Liz Cullis's cash book. We will now go on to use the cash book to demonstrate how double-entry works.

BPP
PROFESSIONAL EDUCATION

8 Double entry

8.1 Recap

Remember every financial transaction gives rise to two accounting entries, one a debit and the other a credit.

DEBIT	CREDIT
To own/have	To owe
↓	↓
AN ASSET INCREASES eg new office furniture	AN ASSET DECREASES eg pay out cash
CAPITAL/ A LIABILITY DECREASES eg pay a creditor	CAPITAL/A LIABILITY INCREASES eg buy goods on credit
INCOME DECREASES eg cancel a sale	INCOME INCREASES eg make a sale
AN EXPENSE INCREASES eg incur advertising costs	AN EXPENSE DECREASES eg cancel a purchase
Left hand side	**Right hand side**

8.2 Cash transactions: double entry

The cash book is a good starting point for understanding double entry. Remember:

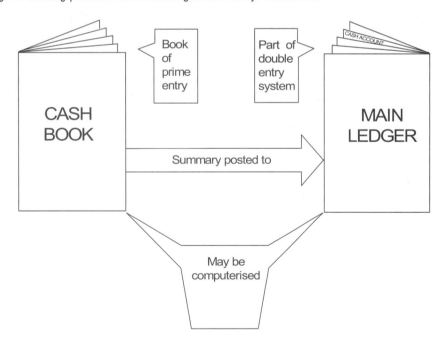

Here are the main cash transactions.

Cash transactions	DR	CR
Sell goods for cash	Cash	Sales
Buy goods for cash	Purchases	Cash
Pay an expense	Expense a/c	Cash

Example: Double entry for cash transactions

In the cash book of a business, the following transactions have been recorded.

   (a)   A cash sale (ie a receipt) of £200
   (b)   Payment of a rent bill totalling £150
   (c)   Buying some goods for cash at £100
   (d)   Buying some shelves for cash at £200

How would these four transactions be posted to the ledger accounts? For that matter, which ledger accounts should they be posted to? Don't forget that each transaction will be posted twice, in accordance with the rule of double entry.

Solution

   (a)   The two sides of the transaction are:

        (i)   Cash is received, increasing the asset (**debit** entry in the cash account)
        (ii)   Sales increase by £200, increasing income (**credit** entry in the sales account)

CASH ACCOUNT

	£		£
Sales a/c	200		

SALES ACCOUNT

	£		£
		Cash a/c	200

        (Note how the entry in the cash account is cross-referenced to the sales account and vice-versa. This enables a person looking at one of the accounts to trace where the other half of the double entry can be found.)

   (b)   The two sides of the transaction are:

        (i)   Cash is paid, decreasing the asset (**credit** entry in the cash account)
        (ii)   Rent expense increases by £150 (**debit** entry in the rent account)

CASH ACCOUNT

	£		£
		Rent a/c	150

RENT ACCOUNT

	£		£
Cash a/c	150		

(c) The two sides of the transaction are:

(i) Cash is paid (**credit** entry in the cash account)

(ii) Purchases increase by £100 (**debit** entry in the purchases account)

CASH ACCOUNT

	£		£
		Purchases a/c	100

PURCHASES ACCOUNT

	£		£
Cash a/c	100		

(d) The two sides of the transaction are:

(i) Cash is paid (**credit** entry in the cash account)

(ii) Assets – in this case, shelves – increase by £200 (**debit** entry in shelves account)

CASH ACCOUNT

	£		£
		Shelves a/c	200

SHELVES (ASSET) ACCOUNT

	£		£
Cash a/c	200		

If all four of these transactions related to the same business, the **summary cash account** of that business would end up looking like this.

CASH ACCOUNT

	£		£
Sales a/c	200	Rent a/c	150
		Purchases a/c	100
		Shelves a/c	200

Activity 2.2

In the cash book of Joanne's business, the following transactions have been recorded on 7 April 20X7.

(a)   A cash sale (ie a receipt) of £600
(b)   Payment of rent totalling £4,500 (no invoice was received)
(c)   Buying some goods for cash at £3,000
(d)   Buying some shelves for cash at £6,000

Task

Draw the appropriate ledger ('T') accounts and show how these four transactions would be posted to them.

8.3 Credit transactions: double entry

Not all transactions are settled immediately in cash.

(a)   A business usually purchases goods from its suppliers on **credit terms**, so that the suppliers are **creditors** of the business until payment in cash.

(b)   A business usually grants credit terms to its customers who are then **debtors** of the business.

Clearly no entries can be made in the cash book when a credit transaction occurs, because initially no cash has been received or paid. Where then can the details of the transactions be entered?

The solution to this problem is to use ledger accounts for debtors and creditors.

CREDIT TRANSACTIONS	DR	CR
Sell goods on credit terms	Debtors	Sales
Receive cash from debtor	Cash	Debtors
Net effect = cash transaction	Cash	Sales
Buy goods on credit terms	Purchases	Creditors
Pay cash to creditor	Creditors	Cash
Net effect = cash transaction	Purchases	Cash

The net effect in the ledger accounts is the same as for a cash transaction – the only difference is that there has been a time delay during which the debtor/creditor accounts have been used.

Example: Credit transactions

Recorded in the sales day book and the purchase day book are the following transactions.

(a)   The business sells goods on credit to a customer Mr A for £2,000.
(b)   The business buys goods on credit from a supplier B Ltd for £100.

How and where are these transactions posted in the ledger accounts?

Solution

(a)   DEBTORS ACCOUNT

	£		£
Sales a/c	2,000		

SALES ACCOUNT

	£		£
		Debtors account (Mr A)	2,000

(b)   CREDITORS ACCOUNT

	£		£
		Purchases a/c	100

PURCHASES ACCOUNT

	£		£
Creditors a/c (B Ltd)	100		

Example continued: When cash is paid to creditors or by debtors

Suppose that, in the example above, the business paid £100 to B Ltd one month after the goods were acquired. The two sides of this new transaction are:

(a) Cash is paid (**credit** entry in the cash account).

(b) The amount owing to creditors is reduced (**debit** entry in the creditors account).

CASH ACCOUNT

	£		£
		Creditors a/c (B Ltd)	100

CREDITORS ACCOUNT

	£		£
Cash a/c	100		

If we now bring together the two parts of this example, the original purchase of goods on credit and the eventual settlement in cash, we find that the accounts appear as follows.

CASH ACCOUNT

	£		£
		Creditors a/c	100

PURCHASES ACCOUNT

	£		£
Creditors a/c	100		

CREDITORS ACCOUNT

	£		£
Cash a/c	100	Purchases a/c	100

The **two entries in the creditors account cancel each other out**, indicating that no money is owing to creditors any more. We are left with a credit entry of £100 in the cash account and a debit entry of £100 in the purchases account. These are exactly the entries which would have been made to record a **cash** purchase of £100.

Similar reasoning applies when a **customer settles his debt**. In the example above, when Mr A pays his debt of £2,000 the two sides of the transaction are:

- Cash is received (debit entry in the cash account)
- The amount owed by debtors is reduced (credit entry in the debtors account)

CASH ACCOUNT

	£		£
Debtors a/c (Mr A)	2,000		

DEBTORS ACCOUNT

	£		£
		Cash a/c	2,000

The accounts recording this sale to, and payment by, Mr A now appear as follows.

CASH ACCOUNT

	£		£
Debtors a/c	2,000		

SALES ACCOUNT

	£		£
		Debtors a/c	2,000

DEBTORS ACCOUNT

	£		£
Sales a/c	2,000	Cash a/c	2,000

The **two entries in the debtors account cancel each other out**, while the entries in the cash account and sales account reflect the same position as if the sale had been made for cash.

Activity 2.3

Identify the debit and credit entries in the following transactions.

(a)   Bought a machine on credit from A, cost £8,000
(b)   Bought goods on credit from B, cost £500
(c)   Sold goods on credit to C, value £1,200
(d)   Paid D (a creditor) £300
(e)   Collected £180 from E, a debtor
(f)   Paid wages £4,000
(g)   Received rent bill of £700 from landlord G
(h)   Paid rent of £700 to landlord G
(i)   Paid insurance premium £90

Activity 2.4

Joanne's business, which is not registered for VAT, has the following transactions.

(a)   The sale of goods on credit
(b)   Credit notes to credit customers upon the return of faulty goods
(c)   Daily cash takings paid into the bank

Task

For each transaction identify clearly:

(a)   The original document(s)
(b)   The book of prime entry for the transaction
(c)   The way in which the data will be incorporated into the double entry system

Tutorial note. We have used the terms debtors account and creditors account for simplicity, while introducing the subject. However the debtors account is also called the **sales ledger control account** and the creditors account the **purchase ledger control account**. This is the terminology used by the AAT and will be used throughout the rest of this text.

9 Posting from the day books

9.1 Sales day book to sales ledger (debtors) control account

Earlier we used four transactions entered into the sales day book.

SALES DAY BOOK

Date 20X7	Invoice	Customer	Sales ledger folios	Total amount invoiced £	Boot sales £	Shoe sales £
Jan 10	247	James Ltd	SL 14	105.00	60.00	45.00
	248	Steptoe & Son	SL 8	86.40	86.40	
	249	Talbot & Co	SL 6	31.80		31.80
	250	John Silvertown	SL 9	1,264.60	800.30	464.30
				1,487.80	946.70	541.10

How do we post these transactions to the main ledger, and which accounts do we use in the main ledger?

We would post the total of the **total amount invoiced column** to the **debit** side of the **sales ledger control account**. The **credit** entries would be to the different **sales accounts,** in this case, boot sales and shoe sales.

SALES LEDGER CONTROL ACCOUNT

	£		£
Boot sales	946.70		
Shoes sales	541.10		
	1,487.80		

BOOT SALES

	£		£
		Sales ledger control	946.70

SHOE SALES

	£		£
		Sales ledger control	541.10

That is why the analysis of sales is kept, and why we analyse items in others books of prime entry.

So how do we know how much we are owed by individual debtors? We keep two sets of accounts running in parallel – the **sales ledger control account** in the main ledger and the memorandum **sales ledger** (individual debtor accounts).

> **REMEMBER!**
>
> **Only the sales ledger control account is actually part of the double-entry system. Individual** debtors' transactions are posted to the sales ledger from the sales day book (see Chapter 4).

9.2 Purchase day book to purchase ledger (creditors) control account

Here is the page of the purchase day book which we saw in Section 5.1.

PURCHASE DAY BOOK

Date	Supplier	Purchase ledger folio)	Total amount invoiced	Purchases	Expenses
20X7			£	£	£
Mar 15	Sugar & Spice	PL 31	315.00	315.00	
	F Seager	PL 46	29.40	29.40	
	ABC	PL 42	116.80		116.80
	Shabnum Rashid	PL 12	100.00	100.00	
			561.20	444.40	116.80

This time we will post the total of the total amount invoiced column to the credit side of the purchase ledger control account in the main ledger. The debit entries are to the different expense account, in this case purchases and electricity.

PURCHASE LEDGER CONTROL ACCOUNT

	£		£
		Purchases	444.40
		Electricity	116.80
			561.20

PURCHASES

	£		£
Purchase ledger control	444.40		

ELECTRICITY

	£		£
Purchase ledger control	116.80		

Again, we keep a separate record of how much we owe individual creditors by keeping two sets of accounts running in parallel – **the purchase ledger control account** in the main ledger, part of the double-entry system, and the memorandum **purchase ledger** (individual creditors' accounts). We enter individual creditors' transactions in their purchase ledger account from the purchase day book (see Chapter 5).

9.3 Section summary

CREDIT TRANSACTIONS	DR		CR	
	Memorandum	*Main ledger**	*Main ledger**	*Memorandum*
Sell goods to John Silvertown	Sales ledger: John Silvertown	Sales ledger control a/c	Sales	–
Receive cash from John Silvertown	–	Cash a/c	Sales ledger control a/c	Sales ledger: John Silvertown
Buy goods from Sugar & Spice	–	Purchases	Purchase ledger control a/c	Purchase ledger: Sugar & Spice
Pay cash to Sugar & Spice	Purchase ledger: Sugar & Spice	Purchase ledger control a/c	Cash a/c	–

*Individual transactions included in **totals** posted from books of prime entry.

Now you do some work! Have a go at these activities.

Activity 2.5

Joanne Smith is a sole trader. The various accounts used in her business are held in a cash book, a sales ledger, a purchase ledger and a main ledger.

The following transactions take place.

(a)   A cheque is issued to P Jones for £264 in payment for goods previously purchased on credit._

(b)   An invoice for £850 is received from Davis Wholesalers Ltd relating to the supply of goods on credit.

(c)   A credit note for £42 is received from K Williams in respect of goods returned.

(d)   New fixtures costing £5,720 are purchased from Fixit Stores and paid for by cheque.

(e)   An invoice for £25 relating to the delivery of the fixtures is received from Fixit Stores and settled immediately by cheque.

(f)   G Cullis sells £85 of goods to Joanne Smith for cash.

(g)   An invoice is issued to R Newman for £340 relating to the purchase by him of goods on credit.

(h)   An insurance premium of £64 is paid to Insureburn Ltd by cheque.

(i)   A cheque for £40 received previously from J Baxter, a credit customer, is now returned unpaid by the bank.

Task

For each transaction in Joanne Smith's books identify clearly:

(a)   The name of the main ledger account to be debited

(b)   The name of the main ledger account to be credited

(c)   Details of any postings to the memorandum accounts.

Present your answer in the form of a table as follows.

Account to be debited	Accounted to be credited	Memorandum
(a)		
(b)		
etc		

Activity 2.6

Joanne's business has the following transactions.

(a)   The purchase of goods on credit
(b)   Allowances to credit customers upon the return of faulty goods
(c)   Refund from petty cash to an employee of an amount spent on entertaining a client

Task

For each transaction identify clearly:

(i)   The original document(s)
(ii)   The book of prime entry for the transaction
(iii) The way in which the data will be incorporated into the double entry system

Key learning points

☑ Business transactions are initially recorded on **source documents**. Records of the details on these documents are made in books of prime entry.

☑ The main **books of prime entry** are as follows.

- Sales day book/sales returns day book
- Purchase day book/purchase returns day book
- Journal
- Cash book
- Petty cash book

☑ Most accounts are contained in the **main ledger** (or general or nominal ledger).

☑ The rules of double entry state that every financial transaction gives rise to **two accounting entries**, one a debit, the other **a credit**. It is vital that you understand this principle.

☑ A **debit** is one of:

- An increase in an asset
- An increase in an expense
- A decrease in a liability

☑ A **credit** is one of:

- An increase in a liability
- An increase in income
- A decrease in an asset

☑ The **sales ledger** and **purchase ledger** are **subsidiary ledgers** which contain memorandum accounts for each individual debtor and creditor. They do not (usually) form part of the double entry system.

Quick quiz

1   What are books of prime entry?

2   What is recorded in the sales day book?

3   Does a debit entry on an asset account increase or decrease the asset?

4   What is the double entry when goods are sold for cash?

5   What is the double entry when goods are purchased on credit?

Answers to quick quiz

1   Books of prime entry record all the documented transactions undertaken by the business.

2   The sales day book records the invoices sent out to customers each day.

3   It increases the asset balance.

4   Debit Cash; Credit Sales.

5   Debit Purchases; Credit Purchase ledger control account.

chapter 3

From ledger accounts to initial trial balance

Contents

1 The problem

How do we get from the ledger accounts to the trial balance, which is the stage before the final accounts? What is the purpose of a trial balance?

How do we account for VAT, the journal and computerised accounting systems?

2 The solution

We have touched on VAT very briefly in Chapter 1. In this chapter, we look at the accounting entries for VAT in detail.

The journal is used for making adjustments to the accounts.

The initial trial balance uses the fact that total debits should equal total credits to check that the double entry is correct.

Computerised accounting systems are no different from manual ones, they use the same double entry principles.

3 Accounting for VAT

In this section, we will outline how VAT is accounted for. (The principles will be similar for most types of sales tax, in most countries, although the rates may differ.)

3.1 Sales revenue

VAT charged is not kept – it is paid back to Customs & Excise. It follows that the **record of sales revenue should not include VAT.**

Example: Accounting for output vat

If a business sells goods for £600 + £105 VAT, ie for £705 gross price, the sales account should only record the £600 excluding VAT. The accounting entries for the sale would be as follows.

DEBIT	Cash **or** sales ledger control	£705	
CREDIT	Sales		£600
CREDIT	VAT account (output VAT)		£105

3.2 Purchases and expenses

Input VAT paid on purchases is not shown as a cost of the business – if it is reclaimed from C&E. However, input VAT is included in purchases if it is **not recoverable**.

(a)   If input VAT is **recoverable**, the cost of purchases should exclude the VAT. If a business purchases goods on credit for £400 + recoverable VAT £70, the transaction would be recorded as follows.

DEBIT	Purchases	£400	
DEBIT	VAT account (input VAT)	£70	
CREDIT	Purchase ledger control		£470

(b)   If the input VAT is **not recoverable**, the cost of purchases must include the tax, because it is the business itself which must bear the cost of the tax.

DEBIT	Purchases	£470	
CREDIT	Purchase ledger control		£470

3.3 When is VAT accounted for?

VAT is accounted for when it first arises – when recording credit purchases/sales in credit transactions, and when recording cash received or paid in cash transactions.

3.3.1 VAT in credit transactions

For credit sales the total amount invoiced, including VAT, will be recorded in the **sales day book**. The analysis columns separate the VAT from sales income as follows.

Date	Total	Sales income	VAT
	£	£	£
Johnson & Co	2,350	2,000	350

Supplier invoices are recorded in total, including VAT, in the **purchase day book**. The analysis columns separate the recoverable input VAT from the purchase cost as follows.

Date	Total	Purchase cost	VAT
	£	£	£
Mayhew (Merchants)	564	480	84

When debtors pay, or creditors are paid, there is no need to show the VAT in an analysis column of the cash book, because the VAT was recorded **when the sale or purchase was made, not when the debt was settled**.

3.3.2 VAT in cash transactions

VAT charged on **cash sales** or VAT paid on **cash purchases will be analysed in a separate column of the cash book**. Output VAT, having arisen from the cash sale, must be credited to the VAT account. Similarly, input VAT paid on cash purchases must be debited to the VAT account.

3.4 The VAT account

The VAT paid to or recovered from the authorities each quarter is the **balance on the VAT account**. This is the **control account** to which these items are posted.

- The total input VAT in the purchases day book (**debit**)
- The total output VAT in the sales day book (**credit**)
- VAT on cash sales (**credit**)
- VAT on cash purchases (**debit**)

Example : VAT account

John Seager is registered for VAT.

(a) He is invoiced for input VAT of £175 on his credit purchases.

(b) He charges £450 VAT on his credit sales.

(c) He makes cash purchases including VAT of £22.30.

(d) He makes cash sales including VAT of £61.07.

Write up the VAT account.

Solution

VAT ACCOUNT

	£		£
Purchase day book (input VAT)	175.00	Sales day book (output VAT)	450.00
Cash (input VAT)	22.30		
		Cash (output VAT)	61.07
Balance c/d (owed to Customs & Excise)	313.77		
	511.07		511.07

When calculating VAT, VAT is always **rounded down** to the nearest penny.

Payments to, or refunds from, Customs and Excise do not usually coincide with the end of the accounting period of a business. At the accounting date there will be a VAT account balance.

If this balance is for an amount **payable to** Customs and Excise, it is an outstanding **creditor** for VAT.

Occasionally, a business will be **owed money** by Customs and Excise. In this case, the VAT refund owed by Customs and Excise is an outstanding **debtor** for VAT.

Activity 3.1

Joanne Smith runs a shop selling books, which are zero rated for value added tax (VAT), and other goods on which standard rate VAT is chargeable at 17½%. No special retail scheme is operated and sales are all made in cash to the general public.

On 7 June 20X7, sales transactions were made with gross values (ie including VAT where applicable) as follows.

Customer number	Gross sales value £	Sales type*
1	72.06	1
2	48.00	2
3	4.25	2
3	11.70	1
4	− 19.20 (refund)	2
5	92.50	2
6	100.00	2
7	58.80	2
7	42.97	1
8	7.99	2
9	52.88	2
9	− 8.40 (refund)	1
10	23.50	2
	487.05	

* 1 = books; 2 = other goods

Tasks

(a) Calculate the amount of VAT arising from the day's sales and refund transactions for which Balvinder must account to HM Customs & Excise.

(b) State the ledger accounting entries to be made to record the transactions.

Tutorial note. To calculate VAT on a gross price, use: $VAT = \dfrac{Gross}{117.5\%} \times 17.5\%$.

3.5 Summary

CREDIT TRANSACTIONS	DR		CR	
	Memorandum	Main ledger	Main ledger	Memorandum
Sell goods on credit	Sales ledger 117.50	Sales ledger control 117.50	Sales 100.00 VAT 17.50	–
Receive cash in settlement	–	Cash 117.50	Sales ledger Control 117.50	Sales ledger 117.50
Buy goods on credit	–	Purchases 100.00 VAT 17.50	Purchase ledger Control 117.50	Purchase ledger 117.50
Pay cash in settlement	Purchase ledger 117.50	Purchase ledger control 117.50	Cash 117.50	–

CASH TRANSACTIONS					
Sell goods for cash	–	Cash 117.50	Sales 100.00		–
			VAT 17.50		
Buy goods for cash	–	Purchases 100.00	Cash 117.50		–
		VAT 17.50			

4 The journal

One of the books of prime entry is the journal.

4.1 The journal

The **journal** is a record of unusual movements between accounts. It records any double entries made which do not arise from the other books of prime entry.

Whatever type of transaction is being recorded, the **format of a journal entry** is:

Date		Folio		
			£	£
DEBIT	Account to be debited		X	
CREDIT	Account to be credited			X
Narrative to explain the transaction				

The ledger accounts are adjusted to include the transactions listed in the journal.

A narrative explanation **must** accompany each journal entry. It is required for audit and control, to indicate the purpose and authority of every transaction which is not first recorded in a book of prime entry.

Example: Journal entries

The following is a summary of the transactions of the Manon Beauty Salon of which David Blake is the sole proprietor.

1 October	Put in cash of £5,000 as capital
	Purchased brushes, combs , clippers and scissors for cash of £485
	Purchased hair driers from Juno Ltd on credit for £240
30 October	Paid three months rent to 31 December of £500
	Collected and paid in to the bank takings of £1,000
31 October	Gave Mrs Sweet a perm and manicure on credit for £100.

Show the transactions by means of journal entries.

Solution

JOURNAL

			£	£
1 October	DEBIT	Cash	5,000	
	CREDIT	David Blake: capital account		5,000
	Initial capital introduced			
1 October	DEBIT	Brushes, combs and scissors account	485	
	CREDIT	Cash		485
	The purchase for cash of brushes etc as fixed assets			
1 October	DEBIT	Hair dryer account	240	
	CREDIT	Sundry creditors account *		240
	The purchase on credit of hair driers as fixed assets			
30 October	DEBIT	Rent account	500	
	CREDIT	Cash		500
	The payment of rent to 31 December			
30 October	DEBIT	Cash	1,000	
	CREDIT	Sales (or takings account)		1,000
	Cash takings			
31 October	DEBIT	Sales ledger control account	100	
	CREDIT	Sales account (or takings account)		100
	The provision of a hair-do and manicure on credit			

*Note. Creditors who have supplied fixed assets are included in **sundry creditors**, as distinct from creditors who have supplied raw materials or goods for resale, who are **trade creditors**.

4.2 The correction of errors

The journal is most commonly used to record **corrections to errors that have been made** in writing up the main ledger accounts. Errors corrected by the journal **must be capable of correction by means of a double entry** in the ledger accounts. The error must not have caused total debits and total credits to be unequal.

4.3 Journal vouchers

Journal entries might be logged, not in a single 'book' or journal, but on a separate slip of paper, called a **journal voucher**.

A **journal voucher** is used to record the equivalent of one entry in the journal.

The use of journal vouchers is fairly widespread because:

(a) Certain journal entries are **repetitive** (vouchers can be pre-printed to standardise the narrative of such entries, and to save time in writing them out)

(b) A voucher is able to hold **more information** than a conventional journal record

5 The initial trial balance

There is no foolproof method for making sure that all entries have been posted to the correct ledger account, but a technique which shows up the more obvious mistakes is to prepare a **trial balance** (or list of account balances).

A **trial balance** is a list of ledger balances shown in debit and credit columns.

5.1 Collecting together the ledger accounts

Before you draw up a trial balance, you must have a **collection of ledger accounts**. These are the ledger accounts of Shabnum Rashid, a sole trader.

CASH

	£		£
Capital: Shabnum Rashid	10,000	Rent	4,200
Bank loan	3,000	Shop fittings	3,600
Sales	14,000	Purchase ledger control	7,000
Sales ledger control	3,300	Bank loan interest	130
		Incidental expenses	2,200
		Drawings	1,800
			18,930
		Balancing figure: the amount of cash left over after payments have been made	11,370
	30,300		30,300

CAPITAL (SHABNUM RASHID)

	£		£
		Cash	10,000

BANK LOAN

	£		£
		Cash	3,000

PURCHASES

	£		£
PLC	7,000		

PURCHASE LEDGER CONTROL (PLC)

	£		£
Cash	7,000	Purchases	7,000

RENT

	£		£
Cash	4,200		

SHOP FITTINGS

	£		£
Cash	3,600		

SALES

	£		£
		Cash	14,000
		SLC	3,300
			17,300

SALES LEDGER CONTROL (SLC)

	£		£
Sales	3,300	Cash	3,300

BANK LOAN INTEREST

	£		£
Cash	130		

OTHER EXPENSES

	£		£
Cash	2,200		

DRAWINGS ACCOUNT

	£		£
Cash	1,800		

The first step is to **'balance' each account**.

5.2 Balancing ledger accounts

At the end of an accounting period, a balance is struck on each account in turn. This means that all the **debits** on the account are totalled and so are all the **credits**.

- If the **total debits exceed the total credits** the account has a **debit balance.**
- If the **total credits exceed the total debits** then the account has a **credit balance**.

Let's see how this works with Shabnum Rashid's **cash account**.

Step 1	**Calculate a total** for **both sides** of **each ledger account**.
	Dr £30,300, Cr £18,930
Step 2	**Deduct** the **lower** total **from** the **higher** total.
	£(30,300 – 18,930) = £11,370
Step 3	**Insert the result of Step 2 as the balance c/d** on the side of the account with the lower total. Here it will go on the credit side, because the total credits on the account are less than the total debits.
Step 4	**Check** that the **totals on both sides** of the account are **now the same.**
	Dr £30,300, Cr £(18,930 + 11,370) = £30,300
Step 5	**Insert the amount of the balance c/d as the new balance b/d on the other side of the account**.
	The new balance b/d is the balance on the account. The balance b/d on the account is £11,370 Dr.

In our simple example, there is very little balancing to do.

(a) Both the purchase ledger control account and the sales ledger control account balance off to zero.
(b) The cash account has a debit balance (the new balance b/d) of £11,370 (see above).
(c) The total on the sales account is £17,300, which is a credit balance.

The other accounts have only one entry each, so there is no totalling to do.

5.3 Collecting the balances on the ledger accounts

If the basic principle of double entry has been correctly applied throughout the period, the **credit balances will equal the debit balances** in total. This is illustrated by collecting together the balances on Shabnum Rashid's accounts.

	Debit £	Credit £
Cash	11,370	
Capital		10,000
Bank loan		3,000
Purchases	7,000	
Purchase ledger control	–	–
Rent	4,200	
Shop fittings	3,600	
Sales		17,300
Sales ledger control	–	–
Bank loan interest	130	
Other expenses	2,200	
Drawings	1,800	
	30,300	30,300

The order of the various accounts listed in the **trial balance** does not matter. It is just a method used to test the accuracy of the double entry bookkeeping.

5.4 What if the trial balance shows unequal debit and credit balances?

If the trial balance does not **balance** there must be an **error in recording of transactions in the accounts**.

A **suspense account** is set up to make the trial balance balance. A suspense account is temporary. The errors need to be found and the suspense account cleared.

A trial **balance** will **not** disclose the following types of errors.

Type 1	The **complete omission** of a transaction, because neither a debit nor a credit is made.
Type 2	A posting to the correct side of the ledger, but to a **wrong account** (also called errors of commission).
Type 3	**Compensating errors** (eg debit error of £100 is cancelled by credit £100 error elsewhere).
Type 4	**Errors of principle** (eg cash received from debtors being debited to the debtors control account and credited to cash instead of the other way round).

Example: Trial balance

As at the end of 29 November 20X1, your business High & Mighty has the following balances on its ledger accounts.

Accounts	Balance £
Bank loan	15,000
Cash	13,080
Capital	11,000
Rates	2,000
Purchase ledger control	14,370
Purchases	16,200
Sales	18,900
Sundry creditors	2,310
Sales ledger control	13,800
Bank loan interest	1,000
Other expenses	12,500
Vehicles	3,000

During 30 November the business made the following transactions.

(a) Bought materials for £1,400, half for cash and half on credit
(b) Made £1,610 sales, £1,050 of which were for credit
(c) Paid wages to shop assistants of £300 in cash

You are required to draw up a trial balance showing the balances as at the end of 30 November 20X1.

Solution

Step 1 Put the opening balances into a trial balance, so decide which are debit and which are credit balances.

Account	Debit £	Credit £
Bank loan		15,000
Cash	13,080	
Capital		11,000
Rates	2,000	
Purchase ledger control		14,370
Purchases	16,200	
Sales		18,900
Sundry creditors		2,310
Sales ledger control	13,800	
Bank loan interest	1,000	
Other expenses	12,500	
Vehicles	3,000	
	61,580	61,580

Step 2	Take account of the effects of the three transactions which took place on 30 November 20X1.

			£	£
(a)	DEBIT	Purchases	1,400	
	CREDIT	Cash		700
		Purchase ledger control		700
(b)	DEBIT	Cash	560	
		Sales ledger control	1,050	
	CREDIT	Sales		1,610
(c)	DEBIT	Other expenses	300	
	CREDIT	Cash		300

Step 3	Amend the trial balance for these entries.

HIGH & MIGHTY: TRIAL BALANCE AT 30 NOVEMBER 20X1

	29/11/20X1 DR	29/11/20X1 CR	Transactions DR	Transactions CR	30/11/20X1 DR	30/11/20X1 CR
Bank loan		15,000				15,000
Cash	13,080		(b) 560	700 (a)	12,640	
Capital		11,000		300 (c)		11,000
Rates	2,000				2,000	
Purchase ledger control		14,370		700 (a)		15,070
Purchases	16,200		(a) 1,400		17,600	
Sales		18,900		1,610 (b)		20,510
Sundry creditors		2,310				2,310
Sales ledger control	13,800		(b) 1,050		14,850	
Bank loan interest	1,000				1,000	
Other expenses	12,500		(c) 300		12,800	
Vehicles	3,000				3,000	
	61,580	61,580	3,310	3,310	63,890	63,890

Activity 3.2

Bailey Hughes started trading as a wholesale bookseller on 1 June 20X7 with a capital of £10,000 with which he opened a bank account for his business.

During June the following transactions took place.

June	1	Bought warehouse shelving for cash from Warehouse Fitters Ltd for £3,500
	2	Purchased books on credit from Ransome House for £820
	4	Sold books on credit to Waterhouses for £1,200
	9	Purchased books on credit from Big, White for £450
	11	Sold books on credit to Books & Co for £740
	13	Paid cash sales of £310 from the warehouse shop intact into the bank
	16	Received cheque from Waterhouses in settlement of their account

17 Purchased books on credit from RUP Ltd for £1,000
18 Sold books on credit to R S Jones for £500
19 Sent cheque to Ransome House in settlement of their account
20 Paid rent of £300 by cheque
21 Paid delivery expenses of £75 by cheque
24 Received £350 from Books & Co on account
30 Drew cheques for personal expenses of £270 and assistant's wages £400
30 Settled the account of Big, White

Tasks

(a)   Record the foregoing in appropriate books of prime entry.
(b)   Post the entries to the ledger accounts.
(c)   Balance the ledger accounts where necessary.
(d)   Extract a trial balance at 30 June 20X7.

6 Computerised systems

So far we have looked at the way an accounting system is organised. You should note that all of the books of prime entry and the ledgers may be either **hand-written books** or **computer records.** Most businesses use computers, ranging from one **PC** to huge **mainframe computer systems**.

6.1 Computer activities

All computer activity can be divided into three processes.

Areas	Activity
Input	Entering data from original documents
Processing	Entering up books and ledgers and generally sorting the input information
Output	Producing any report desired by the managers of the business, including financial statements

Activity 3.3

Your friend Lou Dight believes that computerised accounting systems are more trouble than they are worth because 'you never know what is going on inside that funny box'.

Task

Explain briefly why computers might be useful in accounting.

Computers are covered in detail in BPP's text for Unit 21 **Working with Computers.**

6.2 Batch processing and control totals

Batch processing: similar transactions are gathered into batches, then sorted and processed by the computer.

Inputting individual invoices into a computer for processing (**transaction processing**), is time consuming and expensive. Invoices can be gathered into a **batch** and **input and processed all together**. Batches can vary in size, depending on the type and volume of transactions and on any limit imposed by the system on batch sizes.

Control totals are used to ensure there are no errors when the batch is input. They are used to ensure the total value of transactions input is the same as that previously calculated.

Say a batch of 30 sales invoices has a manually calculated total value of £42,378.47. When the batch is input, the computer adds up the total value of the invoices and produces a total of £42,378.47. The control totals agree, therefore no further action is required.

If the control total does **not agree,** then checks have to be carried out until the difference is found. An invoice might not have been entered or the manual total incorrectly calculated.

6.3 Computer processing

The fact that a computer is used makes no difference to the accounting process.

The computer will post amounts to the ledger, as in a manual system. The only difference is that the ledger accounts are hidden inside the computer until accessed on screen or printed out.

Key learning points

☑ When accounting for VAT, remember to **exclude recoverable** VAT from sales and purchases.

☑ A **journal** is a record of unusual movements between accounts. The journal format is:

Date		Folio £	£
DEBIT	Account to be debited	X	
CREDIT	Account to be credited		X

Narrative to explain the transaction

☑ Balances on ledger accounts can be collected on a **trial balance**. The debit and credit balances should be equal.

☑ If the debit and credit balances are not equal, set up a **suspense account**.

☑ A suspense account is **temporary**, while the errors are found and corrected.

☑ **Computer accounting systems** perform the same tasks as manual accounting systems, but they can cope with greater volumes of transactions and process them at a faster rate.

Quick quiz

1   What is the double entry for goods sold on credit which are standard-rated for VAT and whose price, excluding VAT, is £100?

2   Why must a journal include a narrative explanation?

3   A journal can be used to correct errors which cause the total debits and credits to be unequal. True or false?

4   What is the other name for a trial balance?

5   If the total debits in an account exceed the total credits, will there be a debit or credit balance on the account?

6   What types of error will not be discovered by drawing up a trial balance?

7   What are the advantages of batch processing?

Answers to quick quiz

1   Debit Sales ledger control £117.50; Credit Sales £100.00; Credit VAT £17.50.

2   The narrative is required for audit and control, to show the purpose and authority of the transaction.

3   False. The error must be capable of correction by double entry.

4   The trial balance is also sometimes called the 'list of account balances'.

5   There will be a debit balance on the account.

6   There are four types, summarised as: complete omission; posted to wrong account; compensating errors; errors of principle.

7   Batch processing is faster than transaction processing and checks on input can be made using control totals.

chapter 4

The sales ledger

Contents

1 The problem

A business needs to know what each individual customer owes to the business.

- A customer may **query** his account balance

- A business usually sends out **monthly statements** to each customer

- Managers need to check the **credit position** of each customer and ensure that they do not exceed their **credit limit**

- A business needs to **match** payments received to individual invoices

The sales day book does not fulfil these needs, as it is simply a chronological listing of invoices issued. The sales ledger central account is no help either, as it simply shows the total account owing to **all** debtors.

2 The solution

The solution is to have **personal** accounts for each customer, showing the balance owing to the business. The ledger containing all of these personal accounts is called the **sales ledger.**

2.1 Sales ledger postings

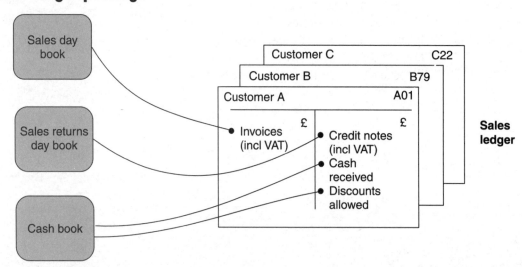

The sales ledger records amounts owing from customers. These are **debtors** and so the sales ledger is an **asset account.**

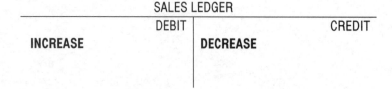

SALES LEDGER	
DEBIT	CREDIT
INCREASE	**DECREASE**

Invoices increase the amount owing and so are **debits**. Credit notes, discounts allowed and amounts received from customers reduce the amount owing and so are **credits.**

3 Personal accounts for credit customers

Each customer account is given a reference or code number (A01, B79, C22 above). This reference (sometimes called the 'sales ledger folio') can be used in the sales day book instead of, or in addition to, the customer name.

Here is an example of how a sales ledger account can be laid out.

	CHEF & CO				A/c no: C124	
Date	*Details*	*£*	*Date*	*Details*		*£*
1.1.X7	Balance b/d	250.00				
10.1.X7	Sales – SDB 48		10.1.X7	Cash		250.00
	(invoice 0249)	343.92	11.1.X7	Balance c/d		343.92
		593.92				593.92
11.1.X7	Balance b/d	343.92				

The opening balance owed by Chef & Co on 11 January 20X7 is now £343.92 instead of £593.92, because of the £250 receipt which came in on 10 January 20X7.

3.1 Personal accounts as memorandum accounts

In manual systems of accounting and in **some** computerised accounting systems, the personal accounts of customers **do not form part of the double entry system of bookkeeping**.

This is because the personal accounts include details of transactions which have already been summarised in day books and posted to ledger accounts.

For example, sales invoices are recorded in the sales account and sales ledger control account. The personal accounts of customers do not then form part of the double entry system: if they did, transactions would be recorded twice over.

3.2 Integrated sales ledger

However, in some computerised systems, the sales ledger is 'integrated' with the **main** ledger.

Instead of being maintained as memorandum accounts reflecting the various customer balances making up the sales ledger control account, individual customers' accounts do form part of the double entry system, and there is **no separate sales ledger control account.**

Instead the computer adds up all the individual sales ledger balances to provide the total debtors' figure.

3.3 Businesses not needing a sales ledger

Surely all but the very smallest businesses will need to maintain a sales ledger? **No, even some very large businesses have no credit sales at all.**

- Chains of supermarkets making sales by cash, cheque or credit card.
- Other businesses selling only to one or two customers eg a defence contractor selling only to a government.

4 Maintaining customer records

A business will keep a personal account for each of its regular customers.

Usually, it will be simpler if there is just one account for each customer. However a business with a number of branches may want to keep separate personal accounts at each branch.

Also if a customer has a number of branches, a business may keep separate account for each branch.

4.1 Opening a new customer account

If an order is received from someone who does not hold a credit account with the business, an account needs to be opened for the new customer.

However, the new account must be **properly authorised**, in accordance with the procedures of the business.

Supplying goods and services on credit involves the **risk that the customer may be unable to pay**.

4.1.1 Credit check

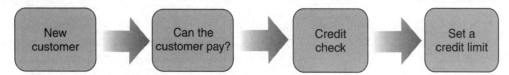

This credit limit will usually be set by a manager or senior employee.

4.1.2 Credit limit

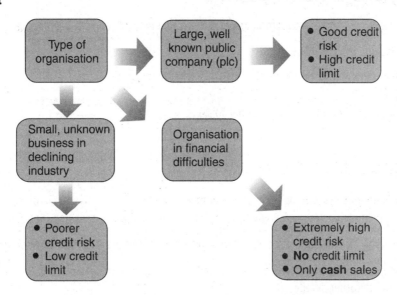

Activity 4.1

Joanne Smith has three new customers. Ali, the bookkeeper, has carried out a preliminary credit check and needs to report back to Joanne. Given the results of the credit checks shown below, complete the grid to show whether you recommend that Joanne give a high, medium or low credit rating or extends no credit at all.

Swansong Ltd	–	old established river cruises company, with good credit record.
Helping Hands Agency	–	newly established cleaning staff agency. Owner has a poor payment record.
Bear and Stag Investments	–	a new investment brokers. Owned by a former City analyst, who is the chief adviser. Excellent credit rating.

Customer	Credit limit			No credit
	High	Medium	Low	

4.1.3 How is a sales ledger account opened?

In a **manual system**, customer details may simply be written on to a new page in the sales ledger.

Customer details will include the following.

- Customer name and address
- Credit limit
- Customer account number (sales ledger folio)
- Normal discount terms (if offered)

Any special terms of business applying to the customer may also need recording, eg special discounts, credit period, sale or return basis and so on.

In a **computerised sales ledger system**, opening an account will be one of the activities involved in maintaining customer records. In a menu-driven system it will be one of the Sales Ledger Processing menu options.

For example, option 1 of the Sales Ledger Processing menu is headed **'Update Account Name/Address'**. Using this option, we can do the following.

- Enter new customer details
- Delete customer accounts which are no longer required
- Amend details of existing customers (eg change of credit limit or address)

The layout of the computer screen for this option can look like the illustration below.

```
SALES LEDGER SYSTEM: CUSTOMER DETAILS

①ACCOUNT CODE:          I 024        CUSTOMER NAME:        Ivory Carpets Ltd  ②

                                     CUSTOMER ADDRESS:
 CONTACT NAME:       Frank Ward
                                                          23 Switchback Rd   ③
 SALES REPRESENTATIVE:   S Morley                         Headingly
                                                          Leeds
                                                          LS3 4PS
 ④ CREDIT LIMIT:        £2,000

 CREDIT PERIOD:        30 days       LAST TRANSACTION      07.02.X4
                                     DATE:

                                     CURRENT BALANCE:      £1,424.67
```

Key

1   **Account code** – a unique code for each customer. To open a new customer account, enter a new customer code and complete the remaining details.

2   **Customer name.**

3   **Customer address** – ensure the full postal address, including post code, is entered. In a fully computerised system, this address will appear on invoices, statements etc. If there is a separate **delivery** address, eg a warehouse away from the main offices, this needs careful noting.

4   **Credit limit** – a computer system will usually **warn the operator** if an invoice will take the customer over the credit limit and allow the option of **cancelling the transaction**. If goods have already been delivered, then a **stop** can be put on the account, until the customer pays off some of the outstanding balance. Sometimes a manager may need to review the account to see if the credit limit needs to be **increased** eg if the customer is a good credit risk, but is simply ordering more from the business due to an increase in its trade.

4.2 Existing customer accounts

Some customers may only make occasional purchases from the business, so that most of the time they do not owe anything to the business.

Once a customer has an account, it makes sense to **keep it open** even if the customer has not made a purchase recently. If the customer wants to make another purchase, the customer's account is still 'active'.

There may be **dormant accounts,** where there have been no transactions for some considerable time. If they are unlikely to be used again, consider closing these accounts. This tidies the ledger and stops old and unnecessary data being produced.

A computerised sales ledger package may include an optional facility for the automatic deletion of zero balances from the sales ledger at the end of a period.

For deleting zero balances	Against deleting zero balances
Save time by deleting 'one-off' sales.	'Zero' accounts may become active again so it is useful to keep them open.
	Avoids having to re-open accounts for customers who return after trying another supplier.
	Keeping all previous customers on the ledger provides a useful customer listing for marketing purposes.

The decision to opt for a facility to delete all zero accounts will depend on the nature of the business.

Activity 4.2

Ali has been reviewing the sales ledger. He finds that two accounts have zero balances. One is for a customer who usually pays cash (in advance). The other is for a customer that clears his account at the end of each month. Should either of these accounts be deleted? Why?

Customer	Delete (Y/N)	Reason

5 Recording transactions in the sales ledger

5.1 Transaction recording

In a **manual system**, the sales ledger is usually written up at the same time as entries are made in the day book or cash book.

In a **computerised system**, transactions may be input directly to customer accounts in the sales ledger (**'transaction processing'**) or alternatively stored as a **transaction file** to form a part of the next updating run.

Example: Sales ledger transactions

Marlon & Co started trading at the beginning of April. During April, the sales day book and the sales returns day book showed the following transactions.

Sales day book

Date	Name	Invoice ref	Net total £ p	VAT £ p	Gross total £ p
2 April	Turing Machinery Ltd	2512	250.00	43.75	293.75
4 April	G Wright	2513	300.00	52.50	352.50
9 April	G Wright	2514	725.00	126.87	851.87
9 April	Turing Machinery Ltd	2515	620.00	108.50	728.50
10 April	Simpsons Ltd	2516	85.00	14.87	99.87
24 April	Simpsons Ltd	2517	1,440.00	252.00	1,692.00
25 April	Simpsons Ltd	2518	242.00	42.35	284.35
25 April	G Wright	2519	1,248.00	218.40	1,466.40
30 April	Totals		4,910.00	859.24	5,769.24

Sales returns day book

Date	Name	Credit note	Net total £ p	VAT £ p	Gross total £ p
23 April	G Wright	0084	220.00	38.50	258.50
25 April	Turing Machinery Ltd	0085	250.00	43.75	293.75
30 April	Totals		470.00	82.25	552.25

During May, the following payments for goods sold on credit were received.

Payments received

		£ p
7 May	Turing Machinery Ltd	728.50
14 May	G Wright	352.50
14 May	Simpsons Ltd	99.87

We need to show the entries as they would appear in the individual sales ledger accounts.

Sales ledger

TURING MACHINERY LTD

Date	Details	£ p	Date	Details	£ p
2 April	Invoice 2512	293.75	25 April	Credit note 0085	293.75
9 April	Invoice 2515	728.50	7 May	Cash book	728.50

G WRIGHT

Date	Details	£ p	Date	Details	£ p
4 April	Invoice 2513	352.50	23 April	Credit note 0084	258.50
9 April	Invoice 2514	851.87	14 May	Cash book	352.50
25 April	Invoice 2519	1,466.40			

SIMPSONS LTD

Date	Details	£ p	Date	Details	£ p
10 April	Invoice 2516	99.87	14 May	Cash book	99.87
24 April	Invoice 2517	1,692.00			
25 April	Invoice 2518	284.35			

Many computerised accounting systems use a **three-column format**, with **debit** items in the left hand column, **credit** items in the middle column and the **balance** in the right hand column.

For example, the entries in G Wright's account in the sales ledger might appear as follows in a three-column format.

Sales ledger	A/c name: G Wright	Debit	Credit	Balance
4 April	2513	352.50		352.50
9 April	2514	851.87		1,204.37
23 April	0084		258.50	945.87
25 April	2519	1,466.40		2,412.27
14 May	Cash book		352.50	2,059.77

Marlon and Co's transactions have been recorded in the sales ledger memorandum accounts, but not in the double entry system.

We have already dealt with the double entry posting in earlier chapters. However, the following example acts as revision.

Example: Posting transactions

The **payments received** will be posted as debits in the **cash account.** (The cash account is an asset account and payments received increase the cash balance.)

CASH ACCOUNT (IN THE MAIN LEDGER)

Date	Details	£ p		£ p
7 May	Turing Mach. Ltd	728.50		
14 May	G Wright	352.50		
14 May	Simpsons Ltd	99.87		

Sales income excluding VAT will be **credits** in the **sales account**.

SALES ACCOUNT

	£ p	Date	Details	£ p
		30 April	Sales day book	4,910.00

Sales returns excluding VAT will be **debits** in the **sales returns account**.

SALES RETURNS ACCOUNT

Date	Details	£ p		£ p
30 April	Sales returns day book	470.00		

VAT on sales and **sales returns** will be **credits** and **debits** respectively in the **VAT account**.

VAT ACCOUNT

Date	Details	£ p			£ p
30 April	Sales returns day book	82.25	30 April	Sales day book	859.24

To complete the double entry, we need to post the **total amounts owed** and the **payments received** to the **debit** and **credit** side respectively of the **sales ledger control account**.

SALES LEDGER CONTROL ACCOUNT (SLCA)

Date	Details	£ p	Date	Details	£ p
30 April	Sales day book total	5,769.24	30 April	Sales returns day book total	552.25
			7 May	Cash book	728.50
			14 May	Cash book	452.37
			31 May	Balance c/d	4,036.12
		5,769.24			5,769.24
1 June	Balance b/d	4,036.12			

Note that in this case the two amounts of cash received on 14 May have been added together to give the **daily total** posted to the total sales ledger control account.

5.1.1 Section summary

Ledger	Source	DEBIT		CREDIT	
Sales ledger (memorandum a/c)	SDB	Sales (inc VAT) [1]	117.50		
	SRDB			Sales returns inc VAT [2]	23.50
	CB			Cash received [3]	94.00
Main ledger (double entry)	SDB	SLCA (inc VAT) [1]	117.50		
	SDB			Sales	100.00
	SDB			VAT	17.50
		Invoices			
	SRDB			SLCA(inc VAT) [2]	23.50
	SRDB	Returns account	20.00		
	SRDB	VAT	3.50		
		Credit notes issued for goods returned			
	CB			SLCA (inc VAT) [3]	94.00
	CB	Cash account	94.00		
		Cash received			

The total entries in the sales ledger memorandum accounts will equal the correspondingly numbered entries in the main ledger shown above.

5.2 Checking the sales ledger recording: reconciling totals to sales ledger control account

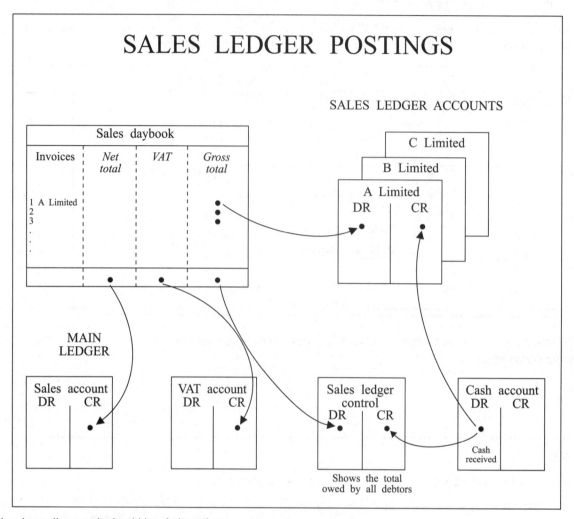

From the above diagram, it should be obvious that:

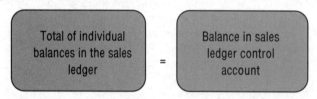

| Total of individual balances in the sales ledger | = | Balance in sales ledger control account |

This provides a **check on the accuracy** of the sales ledger postings. We will deal with this in Chapter 6.

Activity 4.3

You are on work experience and have been asked to help Ali with the sales ledger.

You are presented with the following transactions from Joanne's sales day book and sales returns day book for 1 January 20X7.

SALES DAY BOOK FOLIO 82					
Date	Customer account	Invoice number	Goods value £.00	VAT (17½%) £.00	Total £.00
1/1/X7	001	100	72.35	12.66	85.01
1/1/X7	030	101	83.53	14.61	98.14
1/1/X7	001	102	14.46	2.53	16.99
1/1/X7	132	103	17.20	3.01	20.21
1/1/X7	075	104	104.77	18.33	123.10
1/1/X7	099	105	30.40	5.32	35.72
1/1/X7	001	106	64.97	11.36	76.33
Total 1/1/X7			387.68	67.82	455.50

SALES RETURNS DAY BOOK FOLIO 73						
Date	Customer account	Credit note	Invoice reference	Goods value £.00	VAT (17½%) £.00	Total £.00
1/1/X7	099	C44	89	301.03	52.68	353.71

Tasks

(a)   Post the transactions to the sales ledger accounts provided below.

(b)   Set out the double entry for the transactions shown.

(c)   Comment on any unusual items resulting from your work in (a) and itemise any additional procedures which you consider necessary. Is there anything which should be brought to Ali's attention?

CUSTOMER NAME: *Arturo Aski*

ADDRESS: *94 Old Comedy Street, Vaudeville, 1BR, W. Meds*

CREDIT LIMIT: *£2,200*

Date	Description	Transaction Ref	DR		CR		Balance	
			£	p	£	p	£	p
Brought forward 1/1/X7							2,050	37

CUSTOMER NAME: *Maye West*

ACCOUNT
030

ADDRESS: *1 Vamping Parade, Holywood, Beds, HW1*

CREDIT LIMIT: *£1,000*

Date	Description	Transaction Ref	DR		CR		Balance	
			£	p	£	p	£	p
Brought forward 1/1/X7							69	33

			ACCOUNT 075
CUSTOMER NAME:	Naguib Mahfouz		
ADDRESS:	10 Palace Walk, London NE9		
CREDIT LIMIT:	£1,500		

Date	Description	Transaction Ref	DR		CR		Balance	
			£	p	£	p	£	p
Brought forward 1/1/X7							--------	------

			ACCOUNT 099
CUSTOMER NAME:	Josef Sveik		
ADDRESS:	99 Balkan Row, Aldershot		
CREDIT LIMIT:	£700		

Date	Description	Transaction Ref	DR		CR		Balance	
			£	p	£	p	£	p
Brought forward 1/1/X7							353	71

Date	Description	Transaction Ref	DR		CR		Balance	
			£	p	£	p	£	p
Brought forward 1/1/X7							1,175	80

CUSTOMER NAME: *Grace Chang*

ADDRESS: *Red Dragon Street, Cardiff, CA4*

CREDIT LIMIT: *£1,200*

ACCOUNT *132*

6 Matching cash received

6.1 What is the customer's sales ledger balance made up of?

The **balance** on a sales ledger account shows **how much that customer owes** at any particular time.

Where a customer only makes **occasional purchases**, it is easy to see which invoices are unpaid and so make up the account balance at any particular time.

Example: Sales ledger account

The computer printout below shows all entries in Martlesham Ltd's account in the sales ledger of Domma Ltd, since Martlesham became a customer of Domma in June 20X3.

DOMMA LIMITED A/C NAME: MARTLESHAM LTD			SALES LEDGER SYSTEM A/C NO: M024 DATE: 22.1.X4	
		Debit	*Credit*	*Balance*
30.6.X3	Invoice 7214	472.25		472.25
28.7. X3	Cash received		472.25	0.00
3.8. X3	Invoice 7298	282.00		282.00
21.8. X3	Invoice 7342	424.70		706.70
7.9. X3	Credit note 0141		74.50	632.20
17.9. X3	Cash received		632.20	0.00
10.12. X3	Invoice 7621	845.25		845.25
24.12. X3	Invoice 7710	92.24		937.49
7.1.X4	Cash received		842.25	92.24
20.1.X4	Invoice 7794	192.21		284.45
	Balance			284.45

It should be fairly easy to see that the balance at 22 January 20X4 of £284.45 consists of the amounts due on invoices 7710 and 7794.

A business may have regular customers receiving hundreds of invoices each year.

- Some invoices may be **queried** by the customer and payment withheld until a credit note is issued.

- Payments received from the customer may be in the order that the invoices are **approved** for payment by the customer and not the order in which the invoices are issued.

Clearly, for this customer, it is not so easy to see what invoices remain unpaid at any time.

Why do we need to know exactly which items make up a customer's sales ledger balance?

- Customers must **stick to their allocated credit terms**, and any invoices not paid within this period must be chased up.

- In order to settle any **disagreement** with the customer about the amounts owed.

There are two ways of keeping track of the customer's account.

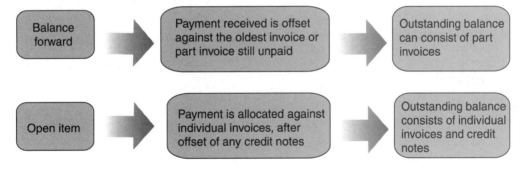

6.2 Matching cash received with invoices and credit notes: open item

6.2.1 Open item method

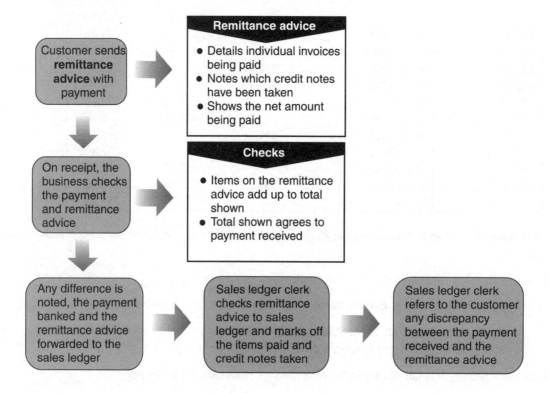

Example: Matching cash received in open item systems

Continuing the above example, Martlesham Ltd sent with their payment of 17 September 20X3 a remittance advice as shown below.

Remittance advice

Heath Ltd
The Green
Menton PR2 4NR

Martlesham Ltd
24 Heath Road
Menton PR7 4XJ

17 September 20X3

Date	Details	Amount/£
3.08.X3	Invoice 7298	+282.00
21.08.X3	Invoice 7342	+424.70
07.09.X3	Credit note 0141	-74.50
	PAYMENT ENCLOSED	632.20

In the sales ledger account below,

DR = debit
CR = credit
* = matched receipt

DOMMA LIMITED   SALES LEDGER SYSTEM
A/C NAME: MARTLESHAM LTD   A/C NO: M024
                                                          DATE: 22.1.X4

		Dr	Cr	Balance	
30.6.X3	Invoice 7214	472.25		472.25	PAID
28.7.X3	Cash received		472.25	0.00	*
3.8.X3	Invoice 7298	282.00		282.00	PAID
21.8.X3	Invoice 7342	424.70		706.70	PAID
7.9.X3	Credit note 0141		74.50	632.20	PAID
17.9.X3	Cash received		632.20	0.00	*
10.12.X3	Invoice 7621	845.25		845.25	PAID
24.12.X3	Invoice 7710	92.24		937.49	
7.1.X4	Cash received		845.25	92.24	*
20.1.X4	Invoice 7794	192.21		284.45	
	Balance			284.45	

To find out the make-up of a customer's balance, it will be cumbersome and unnecessary to keep printing out details of all transactions even after they have been paid. A computer report may be produced showing only those items which remain unpaid (open items). In the case of Martlesham Ltd, this appears as follows on 22 January 20X4.

```
DOMMA LIMITED                                    SALES LEDGER SYSTEM
A/C NAME: MARTLESHAM LTD                              A/C NO: M024
                                                     DATE: 22.1.X4

                                    Dr          Cr        Balance
     24.12.X3        Invoice 7710   92.24                  92.24
     20.1.X4         Invoice 7794   192.21                248.45
                     Balance                             284.45
```

However, the system must continue to keep full records of all transactions.

6.2.2 Unmatched cash in an open item system

Sometimes it is not possible to match cash receipts exactly to outstanding times. This is called **unmatched cash.**

There are different reasons why a receipt may remain unmatched.

- The clerk may **omit to match the cash in error**.

- There may be an **error on the customer's remittance advice** which means that the cash cannot be fully matched.

- The payment may have been **sent without a remittance advice**.

- The customer may have sent a **'round sum' amount** or payment on account (eg exactly £1,000, or 25% of balance) to pay off part of their balance without specifying to which items the amounts relate.

A customer may make round sum payments or payments on account, in accordance with a **schedule of payments** agreed with the customer. Such an agreement may be made if the customer is in **financial difficulties**.

In such a case, it may be better to match receipts with the oldest part of the debt by the **'balance forward'** method, rather than recording it as 'unmatched cash'.

A round sum payment will always result in an amount of cash **remaining unmatched** because it is insufficient to match with the next invoice on the ledger.

Example: Round sum payments or payments on account

Domma Ltd has a customer Hampstead Ltd (Account number H002) with which it has agreed a schedule of payments whereby Hampstead Ltd pays £1,000 at the beginning of each month to clear its remaining debt. £1,000 was paid under this agreement on 2 January 20X4.

At 31 January 20X4, the items remaining unpaid by Hampstead Ltd were shown in Domma Ltd's sales ledger as shown below.

```
DOMMA LIMITED                                    SALES LEDGER SYSTEM
A/C NAME: HAMPSTEAD LTD                              A/C NO:  H002
                                                    DATE: 31.1.X8

                                        Dr          Cr        Balance
10.9.X3          Invoice 7468         649.45                   649.45
24.9.X3          Invoice 7513         424.91                 1,074.36
14.10. X3        Invoice 7581         342.72                 1,417.08
15.11. X3        Invoice 7604         724.24                 2,141.32
2.1.X4           Unmatched cash                   322.90    1,818.42
                 Balance                                    1,818.42
```

We need to show how £1,000 cash received from Hampstead Ltd on 1 February 20X4 will be recorded in the ledger.

The cash available for matching, and the items with which it is matched, are shown below.

	£	£
2.1.X4 payment – unmatched part		322.90
1.2.X4 payment		1,000.00
Cash to be matched		1,322.90
Items to be matched		
Invoice 7468	649.45	
Invoice 7513	424.91	
		(1,074.36)
Cash remaining unmatched		248.54

The remainder of the January payment has now been matched, as has part of the February payment. The balance remaining after invoices 7468 and 7513 have been matched is £248.54, which is not sufficient to match fully with invoice number 7581 for £342.72.

After matching the cash received on 1 February, the ledger shows the account balance as follows.

```
DOMMA LIMITED                                    SALES LEDGER SYSTEM
A/C NAME: HAMPSTEAD LTD                              A/C NO: H002
                                                    DATE: 2.2.X4

                                        Dr          Cr        Balance
14.10.X3         Invoice 7581         342.72                   342.72
15.11.X3         Invoice 7604         724.24                 1,066.96
1.2.X4           Unmatched cash                   248.54      818.42
                 Balance                                      818.42
```

Some sales ledger systems may allow an invoice to be shown as 'part-paid'. In this case, it should be made clear whether an invoice amount shown on a listing is a **part-paid** amount or whether it is instead the full amount of the invoice. This is how a **'balance forward' system,** as opposed to the open item system, works.

Activity 4.4

A long-established customer of Joanne Smith is called Mr Ranjit Singh, of 19 Amber Road, St Mary Cray. His account number is 1124.

Mr Singh's business is a seasonal one but he still requires a steady supply of goods throughout the year.

Mr Singh pays in two different ways. Some invoices he pays off in full. At other times he sends in a payment 'on account' to cover amounts outstanding, but these are not allocated directly to any particular invoice. They are deemed to apply to the earliest uncleared invoices outstanding, unless there is a dispute, or the invoice has had a specific payment made to it.

A computer virus has caused irrecoverable damage to the computer system.

Task

You have to 'reconstruct' the sales ledger for the past few months to discover what Mr Singh owes, as he has requested a statement.

You unearth the following transactions.

Cash receipts (from cash book)

Date	Cash book reference	£	
15/2/X7	004	1,066.05	(Note)
25/3/X7	006	500.00	
15/4/X7	007	500.00	
15/5/X7	031	500.00	
20/5/X7	038	500.00	
20/6/X7	039	500.00	
22/6/X7	042	923.91	
Total receipts		4,489.96	

Note. This covers invoices 236 and 315.

Invoices	Date	Value (inc VAT) £
236	1 January 20X7	405.33
315	2 February 20X7	660.72
317	3 February 20X7	13.90
320	5 February 20X7	17.15
379	21 February 20X7	872.93
443	31 March 20X7	213.50
502	1 May 20X7	624.30
514	15 May 20X7	494.65
521	19 May 20X7	923.91
538	22 May 20X7	110.00
618	1 July 20X7	312.17
619	2 July 20X7	560.73
Total		5,209.29

Credit notes

C32 (against invoice 538)   8 July 20X7   110.00

Tasks

(a)   Post all the transactions to a reconstructed sales ledger. Assume that there was a nil balance at the beginning of the year. Head up the columns: *Date; Transaction reference; Debit; Credit;* and *Balance.*

(b)   Give a breakdown of Mr Singh's balance, stating which invoices are still outstanding.

7 The age analysis of debtors and other reports

7.1 The age analysis of debtors

A business needs a way of knowing whether some of the invoices are **long overdue,** so that those invoices can be followed up with the customer.

If a sales ledger consists of a large number of accounts, it is a long and time-consuming task to go through the details of each account to look for old items.

A lot of time can be saved by summarising the 'age' of the items in the various sales ledger accounts in a single schedule. This is achieved by what is called an **age analysis of debtors**.

An **age analysis of debtors** breaks down the individual balances on the sales ledger according to how long they have been outstanding.

7.2 What does the age analysis look like?

An age analysis of debtors will look very like the schedule illustrated below. The age is calculated according to the **date of the transaction.**

DOMMA LIMITED

AGE ANALYSIS OF DEBTORS AS AT 31.1.X4

Account number	Customer name	Balance	Up to 30 days	Up to 60 days	Up to 90 days	Over 90 days
B004	Brilliant Ltd	804.95	649.90	121.00	0.00	34.05
E008	Easimat Ltd	272.10	192.90	72.40	6.80	0.00
H002	Hampstead Ltd	1,818.42	0.00	0.00	724.24	1,094.18
M024	Martlesham Ltd	284.45	192.21	92.24	0.00	0.00
N030	Nyfen Ltd	1,217.54	1,008.24	124.50	0.00	84.80
T002	Todmorden College	914.50	842.00	0.00	72.50	0.00
Totals		5,311.96	2,885.25	410.14	803.54	1,213.03
Percentage		100%	54.4%	7.7%	15.1%	22.8%

Note. Up to 60 days means older than 30 days but less than 60 days, etc.

You should be able to see how the schedule is prepared by looking at the analysis of the balances of Martlesham Ltd and Hampstead Ltd in Section 6. The unmatched cash has been deducted from the oldest part of the balance.

An age analysis of debtors can be prepared manually or by computer. **Computerisation does make the job a lot easier.**

Activity 4.5

Prepare an aged debtors analysis for the following debtors, ie Tricorn Ltd, Volux Ltd and Yardsley Smith Ltd.

Tricorn Ltd T004		£
Balance b/f	30.6.X3	94.80
Balance c/f	31.1.X4	94.80

Volux Ltd V010		£
15.11.X3	Invoice	500.00
17.11 X3	Invoice	241.25
5.12.X3	Cash received	(500.00)
6 12. X3	Invoice	342.15
23.1.X4	Invoice	413.66
Balance c/f	31.1.X4	997.06

Yardsley Smith & Co Y020		£
1.12.X3	Invoice	520.60
8.12.X3	Invoice	712.30
31.12.X3	Cash received	(1,212.30)
4.1.X4	Invoice	321.17
Balance c/f 31.1.X4		341.77

7.3 How is the age analysis used?

The age analysis is used to **help decide what action to take about older debts**. Going down each column in turn starting from the column furthest to the right and working across, we can see that there are some rather old debts which ought to be investigated.

- **Correspondence** may already exist in relation to some of these items.
- Perhaps some older invoices are still **in dispute**.
- Maybe some debtors are in **financial difficulties**.

From the above age analysis of Domma Ltd's debtors, the relatively high proportion of debts over 90 days (22.8%) is largely due from Hampstead Ltd. Other customers with debts of this age are Brilliant Ltd and Nyfen Ltd.

The age analysis is also used to give a broader picture of the total debtors. If there seems to be a high percentage of older debts, we may question whether the **credit control department**, who chase up slow payers, is performing its role properly.

Sometimes, a column listing **customer credit limits** will appear on the age analysis of debtors. This will make it easy to see which customers (if any) have exceeded or are close to exceeding their current credit limit.

7.4 Other computerised reports

Computerisation of sales ledger processing also allows a number of other reports to be printed out from the information held on the ledger. Access to sales ledger reports may be restricted to authorised staff members, whose password will allow them access.

7.4.1 Other reports

- Sales day book listings
- Statements of account
- VAT analysis
- Sales analysis – by type of product, area, sale representative etc
- List of customer accounts
- Customer mailing lists

A VAT analysis can be useful if the business has sales at different VAT rates. Also if the business **imports or exports goods**, the analysis can be used to prepare the **EU Intrastat** report (showing how much VAT-able supplies were made to other EU countries).

Key learning points

- ☑ The **sales ledger contains the personal accounts** of credit customers of the business.

- ☑ An account must be kept for each customer so that the business always has a full record of how much each customer owes and what items the debt is made up of.

- ☑ A **customer's account** in the sales ledger will **normally show a debit balance:** the customer owes money to the business and is therefore a debtor of the business.

- ☑ Usually **customers' personal accounts** are maintained separately from the main (or 'impersonal') ledger, as **'memorandum' accounts**. Sales ledger postings then do not form part of the double entry in the system of bookkeeping.

- ☑ Instead, a **sales ledger control account** is maintained in the main ledger to **keep track of the total of the amounts** which make up the entries in the individual personal accounts.

- ☑ Opening a **new sales ledger account** requires **authorisation** by a senior official. The amount of credit allowed to each individual customer should be kept **within acceptable limits of risk**.

- ☑ To make it clear exactly what a sales ledger customer's balance is made up of (which invoices remain unpaid), cash received from the customer is matched with the items for which it has been sent as the customer's payment. The customer indicates on the **remittance advice** which items are being paid.

- ☑ The **age analysis of debtors** is useful to a credit controller wishing to decide on which debts to chase up. It also provides a general guide as to whether the debts of a business are being collected quickly enough.

- ☑ Various other useful reports may be printed out from a **computerised sales ledger package**.

Quick quiz

1   What does the sales ledger contain?

2   In manual accounting systems the personal accounts of customers do not form part of the double entry system. True or false?

3   What factors determine the credit limit allocated to a particular customer?

4   How might you check the accuracy of the amounts recorded in the sales ledger?

5   What is the 'open item' method of keeping track of a customer's account?

6   What is the 'balance forward' method?

7   What is the function of an age analysis of debtors?

Answers to quick quiz

1   The personal accounts of customers.

2   True.

3   (i)   The trading record of the customer
    (ii) The industry in which he operates
    (iii) The size of the customer

4   Work out the total of the balances on the individual sales ledger accounts and compare this with the total balance on the sales ledger control account.

5   A method which keeps track of individual items which remain unpaid.

6   Any payment received is simply allocated to the oldest items or part items which remain unpaid.

7   It breaks down the debtor balances on the sales ledger into different periods of outstanding debt.

chapter 5

The purchase ledger

Contents

1 The problem

The purchase day books provide a chronological record of the invoices and credit notes received by a business from all credit suppliers.

However this will not answer all needs.

- If a supplier requests **payment of the full balance due to him**

- To check that the monthly supplier's **statement of account** is correct

- To maintain a **complete record** of the items making up the balance owed to each supplier, so that **appropriate payments** can be made

- To make **monthly payments** covering a number of invoices, rather than each invoice separately

2 The solution

The answer is the individual supplier personal accounts in the **purchase ledger**.

Each personal account shows the amount owed to each supplier.

2.1 Purchase ledger postings

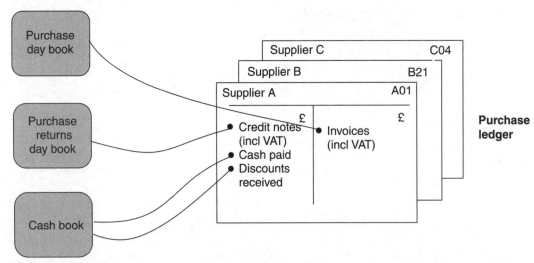

The purchase ledger records amounts due to suppliers. These are **creditors** and so the purchase ledger is a **liability account**.

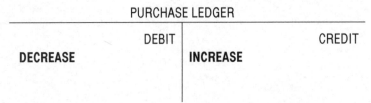

PURCHASE LEDGER

DEBIT	CREDIT
DECREASE	INCREASE

Invoices increase the amount owing and so are **credits**. Credit notes, discounts received and cash paid reduce the liability and so are **debits.**

2.2 Terminology

- Subsidiary ledger (purchase ledger or sales ledger)
- Main ledger (the main double entry records, usually referred to as the general or nominal ledger)
- Integrated ledger (where the subsidiary ledgers form part of the double entry eg in a **computerised system**)

3 Personal accounts for suppliers

An example of a purchase ledger account is shown below.

COOK & CO   PL32

Date 20X2	Details	£	Date 20X2	Detail	£
15 March	Purchase returns PRDB 21	50.00	15 March	Balance b/d	200.00
15 March	Cash CB 44	135.00	15 March	Invoice rec'd PDB 37	315.00
15 March	Discount rec'd CB 44	15.00			
16 March	Balance c/d	315.00			
		515.00			515.00
			16 March	Balance b/d	315.00

3.1 Debit balances in the purchase ledger

If we pay more than £315 to Cook & Co, we will be left with a net debit balance on Cook & Co's personal account. For instance, if we pay £375, there will be a net debit balance of £60. This indicates that the creditor owes us £60.

Debit balances in the purchase ledger are unusual, but they can sometimes arise.

- **Deposit** paid in advance of receipt of the goods
- **Overpayment** of the creditor's balance made in error
- **Credit note** received after full payment has been made of the balance

If debit balances are arising on purchase ledger accounts frequently, some **investigation** may be needed. The occurrence of debit balances could indicate that procedures in the purchase ledger department need to be improved.

3.2 Organisations not needing a purchase ledger

Maintaining a separate purchase ledger is a waste of time for businesses with very few credit purchases. Examples include small shops, clubs and associations. Any credit purchases will be posted direct to the **main ledger accounts**.

3.3 Trade creditors

The purchase ledger contains the personal accounts of creditors for the supply of both goods and services. It will normally cover only the **trade creditors** of the business.

3.3.1 Trade creditors

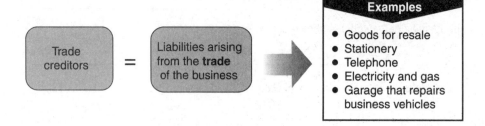

3.4 Other creditors

Other creditors are recorded directly in main ledger accounts. Examples of 'other creditors' include the following.

- **Liabilities to pay wages and salaries**

- **Taxes** (eg PAYE) and other amounts (eg VAT) which are collected by the business on behalf of third parties

- Amounts payable *not* directly related to the main trade of the business, eg purchase of **fixed assets**

Some items of **overhead expenditure** (eg rent and rates) are treated as trade creditors in some businesses, while others treat them as other creditors.

Activity 5.1

(a)   What is the status of a trade creditor in the accounts of a business?

    (i)   An asset
    (ii)   A liability
    (iii)   An expense
    (iv)   An item of revenue

(b)   Which of the following accounts are normally found in a purchase ledger (ie which are trade creditors)?

Accounts	Purchase ledger (Y/N)
(i) Personal accounts for suppliers of subcomponents	
(ii) Inland Revenue	
(iii) Customs & Excise for VAT	
(iv) Suppliers of raw materials	
(v) Bank overdraft	
(vi) Long-term bank loan	
(vii) Telephone expenses	
(viii) Drawings	
(ix) Proprietor's capital	

4 Maintaining supplier records

4.1 Opening a new ledger account for a supplier

Opening a ledger account for a new supplier must be **authorised**. The procedures of a business should specify in detail the **level of authorisation** required.

This is important because frauds sometimes involve putting transactions through a dummy supplier account.

A computerised purchase ledger system needs to be able to create, delete and amend suppliers' details on the **supplier master file**.

In a menu-driven purchase ledger system, an option on the purchase ledger system might produce the following menu.

1. Update account name/address
2. Ledger postings
3. Enquiries
4. Dispute/release
5. Creditors total

Option 1 will enable the user to do the following.

- Enter new supplier details, together with discount and trading terms
- Delete supplier accounts which are no longer required
- Amend details of existing suppliers, eg change of address

Each supplier has a **unique account number** chosen by the purchasing business. This means that any particular supplier can be identified by just the account number.

There may be good reasons for maintaining **more than one account** for a particular supplier, eg he supplies different categories of goods and services.

(a)   A printing business might order its raw materials (paper and ink) from the same company which provides office stationery.

(b)   The different types of purchases are posted to different accounts in the main ledger (eg the **paper and ink** and **stationery accounts)**. So operating different accounts may avoid confusion.

The purchase ledger system should have a facility for recording **suppliers' credit limits**. This warns the user if the total outstanding is near to the credit limit. Payments to the supplier are needed before more orders are placed.

4.2 Deleting and amending existing accounts

Any supplier record no longer required should be **deleted**. It may be possible to specify that a supplier account is automatically deleted if the balance falls to zero.

However, there are good reasons why you should not make use of such a facility.

- Retain supplier records on the ledger for future reference
- Avoid having to create a new supplier record when you start trading again with a supplier whose balance has fallen to zero

However, if a business makes numerous 'one-off' purchases, the facility may help reduce the size of the supplier files and to make the ledger more manageable.

To **amend the supplier record,** enter the account number and alter the particular 'fields' of data concerned eg change of address. Appropriate authorisation will be necessary in order to avoid fraud.

4.3 'Open item' and 'balance forward'

In a computerised purchase ledger package, and in most manual systems, the account may be either an **'open item'** or a **'balance forward'** type account.

- By the **open item method**, cash paid is matched directly against outstanding invoices. At the end of the period (say a month), any invoices remaining unpaid are carried forward to the next period. Most purchase ledger systems are of this type.
- By the **balance forward method**, cash paid is matched against the oldest outstanding invoices. At the end of the period, a balance is carried forward to the next period. A problem of this method is that parts of invoices will be carried forward.

4.4 Dividing the ledger

The purchase ledger may be **divided up into parts**, for administrative convenience. This may reduce the risk of fraud by having different clerks post different parts of the ledger. For example, there might be three purchase ledgers.

Purchase ledger 1, for suppliers with names beginning A-J
Purchase ledger 2, for suppliers with names beginning K-O
Purchase ledger 3, for suppliers with names beginning P-Z

Alternatively, the ledger might be divided by geographical region. The sales ledger may be divided in the same ways.

Activity 5.2

You operate a computerised purchases ledger system, and are offered the following menu.

1	Account name and address update
2	Postings
3	Enquiries
4	Dispute
5	Creditors total

(a) Briefly describe Option 1.
(b) What sort of transactions would you post in Option 2?

Activity 5.3

The following transactions have been posted to a purchase ledger account.

Date	Narrative	Trans ref	Debit £ p	Credit £ p	Balance £ p
Balance at 31/8/X7					NIL
2/9/X7		P901		453.10	453.10
3/9/X7		P902		462.50	915.60
4/9/X7	Cash	C9901	462.50		453.10
5/9/X7		P903		705.90	1,159.00
7/9/X7		P904		25.50	1,184.50
12/9/X7	Cash	C9902	705.90		478.60
15/9/X7		P905		914.30	1,392.90
17/9/X7		P906		692.53	2,085.43
19/9/X7	Cash	C9903	692.53		1,392.90
21/9/X7		P907		805.39	2,198.29
22/9/X7		C9904	914.30		1,283.99
25/9/X7		P908		478.60	1,762.59
28/9/X7	Cash	C9905	805.39		957.20
29/9/X7	Cash	C9906	478.60		478.60
30/9/X7		P909		92.70	571.30
Balance at 30/9/X7					£571.30

Task

At close of business on 30 September 20X7, tell Joanne which invoices are outstanding, applying:

(a) the open item method
(b) the balance forward method

5 Recording transactions in the purchase ledger

In a computer system, accounts can be updated directly (**transaction processing**) or stored on a **transaction file** for a later updating run. Similarly a manual system may be posted daily, weekly or monthly.

5.1 Recording purchases and cash paid

The chart below shows how entries are made in purchase ledger accounts.

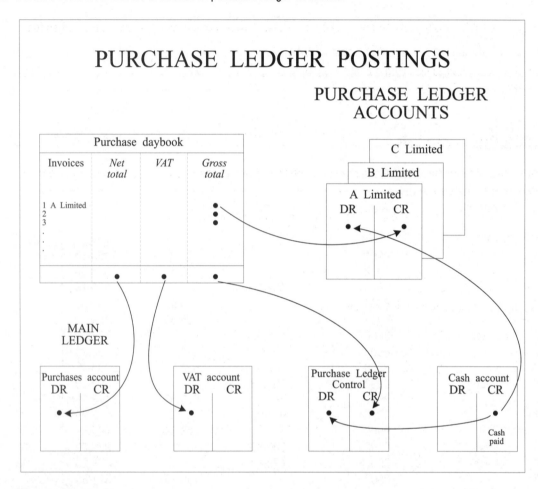

5.1.1 Posting summary

Double entry:		*Debit (DR)*	*Credit (CR)*
Total invoices (incl VAT)	PDB		Purchase ledger control a/c
Net invoices (excl VAT)	PDB	Purchases or expense a/c	
VAT	PDB	VAT a/c	
Cash paid	CB	Purchase ledger control a/c	Cash account
Memorandum:			
Each invoice (incl VAT)			Individual purchases ledger a/c
Each cash payment		Individual purchase ledger a/c	

PROFESSIONAL EDUCATION

5.1.2 Posting purchase returns

Postings of credit notes received are made to the **debit** of the purchase ledger accounts. In the main ledger, the double entry postings are **debit purchase ledger control account** and **credit purchases**.

5.2 Discounts received

Some businesses account for **cash discounts received** from suppliers by a 'memorandum' discounts received column in the cash book.

This is used to **debit** the individual creditors' accounts. The appropriate double entry main ledger entries follow.

		£	£
		£	£
DEBIT	Purchase ledger control account	X	
CREDIT	Discounts received		X

5.3 Retention of records

All purchase invoices and credit notes should be retained and filed after processing in case of query (from the supplier, the management or the auditors).

Where VAT is involved, invoices and credit notes **must be retained for six years**.

Activity 5.4

Joanne's purchase day book includes the following entries.

	Gross	VAT	Net	Purchases	Gas	Stationery
Alfred	1,175.00	175.00	1,000.00	1,000.00		
N. Gas Co	822.50	122.50`	700.00		700.00	
Bertie	587.50	87.50	500.00	500.00		
Stanner supplies	705.00	105.00	600.00			600.00

Joanne made a return to Alfred and the following credit note is in the purchase returns day book.

	Gross	VAT	Net	Purchases	Gas	Stationery
Alfred	293.75	43.75	250.00	250.00		

Tasks

(a) Complete the memorandum purchase ledger accounts, using the 'T' accounts below.
(b) Complete the double entry, using the 'T' accounts below.

ALFRED		BERTIE	
£	£	£	£

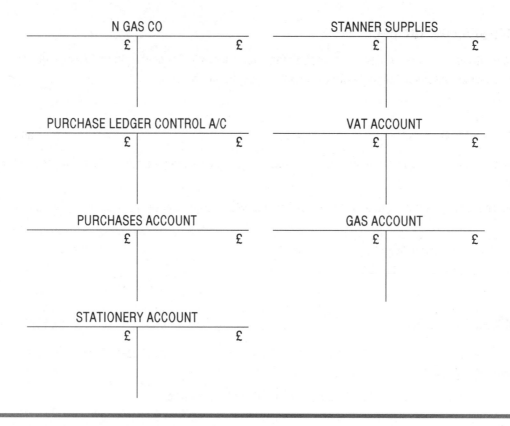

N GAS CO		STANNER SUPPLIES	
£	£	£	£

PURCHASE LEDGER CONTROL A/C		VAT ACCOUNT	
£	£	£	£

PURCHASES ACCOUNT		GAS ACCOUNT	
£	£	£	£

STATIONERY ACCOUNT	
£	£

6 Payments to suppliers

Payments to suppliers are best made on a **regular basis**, say monthly, as a matter of efficiency.

6.1 Methods of payment

Different methods of payment to suppliers are available.

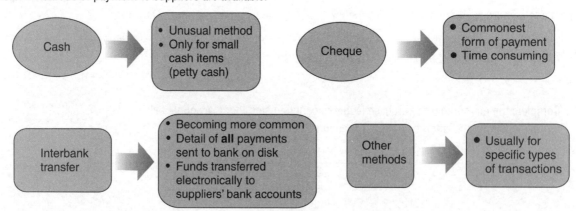

Cash →
- Unusual method
- Only for small cash items (petty cash)

Cheque →
- Commonest form of payment
- Time consuming

Interbank transfer →
- Becoming more common
- Detail of **all** payments sent to bank on disk
- Funds transferred electronically to suppliers' bank accounts

Other methods →
- Usually for specific types of transactions

6.2 Selecting items for payment

Deciding when and who to pay is a key function of a business's management and only a senior person should decide.

All systems	Computerised purchase ledger system
The items for payment may be selected manually.	A '**suggested payments**' listing may show how much should be paid to which suppliers, based on settlement days and any discounts offered. This listing needs to be checked manually in case there are any reasons to make a different payment from that 'suggested'.
If **queries** on any invoices are outstanding the invoice should not be paid until the query has been settled. (The invoice should be kept in a separate 'queried invoices' file.)	There may be a facility to 'flag' items which should not be paid for the time being. The 'flag' will need to be 'released' when the dispute is settled, so that payment can be made.
It may be desirable to take the full period of credit from each supplier.	The number of days before settlement can be recorded for each supplier. There may be an option of making automatic payments and this will list all items which are now due to be paid. This list will *exclude*: • Items which have not yet reached their settlement date • Items which are 'in dispute'

6.3 Computer cheques and remittance advices

A computerised purchase ledger system may offer the option of **printing cheques for payments to suppliers.** Special cheque stationery is needed.

A **remittance advice** is normally sent with each payment to tell the supplier what the payment is for. This too may be produced by a computerised purchase ledger system.

REMITTANCE ADVICE

KT Electronics	R&B Sound Services Ltd
4 Reform Road	Belton Estate
Wokingham	Peterborough
Berkshire	PE4 4DE

30/06/X3
Your ref: RBS/2011

Account number: 427424

Date	Details	Amount/£
08/05/X3	Invoice 202481	624.60
21/05/X3	Invoice 202574	78.40
24/05/X3	Credit note C40041	(62.20)
	Payment enclosed for	640.80

6.4 Checks over payments

It is important for a business to have **procedures to ensure that only valid payments are made** – ie only the payments which *should* be made by the business.

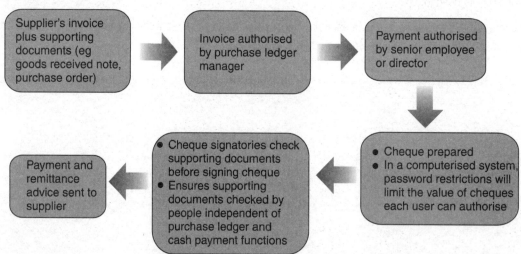

Automatic payment methods in a large organisation may include **mechanical signature of cheques by computer**. If such a system is used, there is not the same check on individual payments and there will have to be strong checks over whether purchase ledger balances are correct to ensure that wrong payments are not made.

If automated electronic payments methods (such as **BACS**) are used, there will need to be special procedures to ensure that all payments included on the tape submitted to BACS are properly authorised.

Sometimes, the usual payment method may need to be bypassed. For example, a special **manual payment** may be needed if the credit limit is exceeded. Proper checks will be needed in such cases and high level authorisation obtained.

7 The age analysis of creditors and other reports

7.1 The age analysis of creditors

An **age analysis of creditors** is produced in a similar way to the age analysis of debtors. It is a listing showing how old the creditor balances are.

The age analysis of creditors highlights any supplier accounts which are **long overdue**, for whatever reason.

The totals of the age analysis indicate the **'age profile'** of creditors' accounts. This profile is used by business managers to check whether the business would be better off paying creditors a little later in order to improve its cash flow position.

7.2 Other reports

Other reports which a computerised purchase ledger package is able to print out will be very similar to those produced from a sales ledger package, the more important of which were outlined in Chapter 4.

Access to purchase ledger reports will normally be restricted by **password**.

Activity 5.5

What, briefly, is the significance of a *creditors'* age analysis?

Activity 5.6

Can you list the main types of report other than the age analysis of creditors?

8 Contra entries with the sales ledger

Sometimes, a business **purchases goods from** and **sells goods to** the same person on credit.

- **Purchase** invoices will be entered in the **purchase day book** and recorded in the supplier's individual account in the purchase ledger

- **Credit sales** invoices are entered in the **sales day book** and subsequently recorded in the customer's individual account in the sales ledger

Even though the supplier and the customer are the same person, he will have a **separate account in each ledger**. If A owes B £200 for purchases and B owes A £350 for credit sales, the net effect is that B owes A £150. However, in the books of A, there will be the following entries.

- A creditor in the purchase ledger – B – for £200
- A debtor in the sales ledger – B – for £350

If A and B decide to settle their accounts by **netting off** their respective debts (and getting B to write a single cheque for the balance of £150), settlement would be made **by a contra entry**.

The contra entries in the accounts of A would be to set off the smaller amount (£200 owed *to* B) against the larger amount (£350 owed *by* B).

(a)   In the *sales ledger* and *purchase ledger*.

DEBIT	Creditor's account (B) purchase ledger – to clear	£200
CREDIT	Debtor's account (B) sales ledger – leaving balance of £150	£200

(b)   In the *main ledger*.

DEBIT	Purchase ledger control account	£200
CREDIT	Sales ledger control account	£200

The contra entries must be made in both the personal accounts for B and also in the purchase ledger and sales ledger control accounts in the main ledger.

Activity 5.7

You are the purchase ledger clerk for Joanne Smith, and the date is 28 August 20X7. The business operates a non-integrated purchase ledger system, ie the purchase ledger is a memorandum account.

The purchase ledger account for a supplier called Kernels Ltd shows the following.

		(Debit)/Credit £	Balance £
01.08.X7	Balance b/f		76.05
01.08.X7	Invoice 20624	42.84	118.89
07.08.X7	Cash	(76.05)	42.84
16.08.X7	Invoice 20642	64.17	107.01
16.08.X7	Invoice 20643	120.72	227.73
16.08.X7	Invoice 20642	64.17	291.90
21.08.X7	Cash	(400.00)	(108.10)
22.08.X7	Invoice 20798	522.18	414.08
24.08.X7	C91004	42.84	456.92
27.08.X7	Invoice 21114	144.50	601.42
27.08.X7	Invoice 21229	42.84	644.26

The following facts came to light.

(a) Kernels Ltd's invoice 21201 for £97.40, dated 23 August 20X7, was misposted to the account of MPV in the purchase ledger.

(b) The cash payment of £400.00 made on 21 August 20X7 relates to another creditor, ASR Ltd.

(c) Item C91004 dated 24 August 20X7 is in fact a credit note.

(d) Invoice 20642 has been posted to the account twice.

(e) Kernels Ltd has a balance of £37.50 in the sales ledger, which is to be set off against its balance in the purchase ledger.

Task

Draw up journal entries for the above items and write up the Kernels Ltd's account accordingly, posting the journal entries to the account.

The journal entries should distinguish between main ledger adjustments and memorandum account adjustments.

Key learning points

☑ The purchase ledger contains the **personal accounts of suppliers** (trade creditors) of the business.

☑ The suppliers' personal accounts provide the business with a full record of how much it owes to each supplier and of what items the debt consists.

☑ A **supplier's account** in the purchase ledger **will normally show a credit balance**: the supplier is owed money by the business and is therefore a creditor of the business.

☑ Other creditors which a business may have include the tax authorities, banks and employees (for any wages and salaries due).

☑ Opening a new purchase ledger account or amending an existing record will require the **authorisation** of a senior official.

☑ A computerised system may use a 'menu' system through which supplier records may be added, deleted or amended. Authorisation may be by way of a **password** known only to authorised employees.

☑ Payments to suppliers should be organised according to the periodic procedures of the business. **Checks and authorisation** are necessary in order to ensure that only valid payments are made.

☑ The **age analysis of creditors** shows the 'age profile' of creditors' balances on the purchase ledger. It indicates how quickly the business is paying off its debts.

☑ A computerised purchase ledger will also allow a number of other reports to be printed out as necessary.

☑ **Contra entries** 'net off' amounts due to and from the same parties in the purchase ledger and sales ledger respectively.

Quick quiz

1   What does the purchase ledger contain?

2   What are trade creditors?

3   Give two examples of 'other creditors'.

4   The purchase ledger may be divided up. Suggest two ways of dividing it.

5   What does the age analysis of creditors do?

6   What does settlement 'in contra' mean?

Answers to quick quiz

1   The personal accounts showing how much is owed to each credit supplier of the business.

2   Liabilities relating to the trade of the business, eg purchases of goods for re-sale.

3   (i)   Wages and salaries
    (ii)   VAT

4   (i)   Alphabetically
    (ii)   Geographically

5   Lists creditors' balances analysed between different 'ages' of debt, eg one month old, two months old etc.

6   An amount due from a customer in the sales ledger is set off against an amount owed to the same person in the purchase ledger, and vice versa.

107

chapter 6

Sales ledger control account

Contents

1 The problem

In Chapter 2 we saw that:

(a)   Sales invoices and cash received are logged in a **day book**

(b)   Each invoice and cash receipt is posted **singly** to an appropriate personal account in the sales ledger

But these personal accounts are for memorandum purposes only and do not form a part of the double entry system.

2 The solution

To record these transactions in the **double entry system** we do not need to deal with each invoice singly. Instead, the day books can be totalled at convenient intervals (eg daily, weekly or monthly) and these total amounts are recorded in the main ledger. For sales invoices, this means an accounting entry is made as follows.

DEBIT	Sales ledger control account	£1,175	
CREDIT	Sales account(s)		£1,000
	VAT account		£175

3 Sales ledger control account

A control account keeps a record of the total value of a number of similar but individual items.

- A sales ledger control account keeps a record of transactions involving all debtors in total.

- The balance on the sales ledger control account at any time will represent the total amount due to the business at that time from its debtors.

A control account is an (impersonal) ledger account which will appear in the main ledger.

3.1 Control accounts and personal accounts

The personal accounts of individual debtors are kept in the sales ledger, and the amount owed by each debtor will be a balance on that **debtor's personal account**. The amount owed by all the debtors together will be the balance on the **sales ledger control account**.

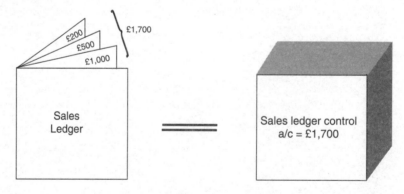

For example, if a business has three debtors, A Ashton who owes £80, B Bolton who owes £310 and C Collins who owes £200, the balances on the various accounts would be:

Sales ledger (personal accounts)

	£
A Ashton	80
B Bolton	310
C Collins	200

All of these balances would be debit balances.

Main ledger: sales ledger control account	590

4 Posting to the sales ledger control account

Typical entries in a sales ledger control account are shown in the example below. The 'folio' reference 'Jnl' in this example indicates that this particular transaction is first **entered** in the **journal** before **posting** to the **control account** and other accounts indicated. The reference SDB is to the sales day book, the reference SRDB is to the sales returns day book and the reference CB is to the cash book.

SALES LEDGER CONTROL ACCOUNT

	Folio	£		Folio	£
Debit balances b/d	b/d	7,000	Credit balances c/d	b/d	200
Sales	SDB	52,390	Cash received	CB	52,250
Dishonoured cheques	Jnl	1,000	Discounts allowed	CB	1,250
Cash paid to clear			Returns inwards from		
credit balances	CB	110	debtors	SRDB	800
Credit balances	c/d	120	Bad debts	Jnl	300
			Debit balances	c/d	5,820
		60,620			60,620
Debit balances	b/d	5,820	Credit balances	b/d	120

Note some points about the various kinds of entry shown above.

Debit entries	Points to note
Debit balances b/d	Most **debtor balances** will be **debit balances**: customers will usually owe money to the business.
Sales	These are the **sales** totals posted periodically from the **sales day book**. The amounts recorded will include VAT, since debtors are due to pay the VAT to us.
Dishonoured cheques	A cheque received will be shown as a credit entry, since we treat it as **cash received**. If a cheque is dishonoured by the debtor's bank, it means that the cheque has 'bounced' and the amount will not be paid to the business. A **debit entry** is necessary to 'reverse' the recording of the cheque as a cash receipt and to reinstate the debt. The cheque has not been paid and the debtor still owes the amount to us. The entry is from the journal, which also updates the cash book.

Debit entries	Points to note
Cash paid by us to clear credit balances	If a customer has a credit balance, **we owe money** to that customer, and we may clear the balance by paying money to the customer. The entry is from the **cash book.**
Credit balances c/d	Any closing credit balances are carried down.
Credit entries	**Points to note**
Credit balances b/d	**Credit balances** in the sales ledger control account can arise, for example, if goods which have already been paid for are **returned**, or if a customer has **overpaid**. Such balances will be unusual.
Cash received	**Cash received from debtors** will be posted from the **cash book.**
Discounts allowed	**Cash discounts allowed** may be recorded in a memorandum column in the cash book. They form a part of the amounts invoiced to customers which we are 'allowing' them not to pay, so a credit entry is needed to cancel that part of amounts invoiced which is being allowed as discount, posted from the **cash book.**
Returns inwards	**Credit notes** for returns inwards must be posted from the **sales returns day book.**
Bad debts	Bad debts written off need to be **cancelled** from the control account by means of a credit entry (debit bad debts account). Usually the source will be the **journal**.
Debit balances c/d	The bulk of sales ledger balances to carry forward will be debit balances.

Activity 6.1

Prepare a specimen sales ledger control account in T account form. Show clearly the information it would contain and the sources of this information.

Activity 6.2

Tick the items below which you would **not** expect to see as individual items in a sales ledger control account.

1   Credit balances on individual debtor accounts
2   Debit balances on individual debtor accounts
3   Cash sales
4   Sales on credit
5   Provision for bad and doubtful debts
6   Settlement discounts allowed
7   Trade discounts received
8   Cash receipts
9   Bad debts written off

10   Sales returns
11   Credit notes received
12   Credit notes issued

5 Comprehensive example: accounting for debtors

This is a good point at which to go through the steps of how transactions involving debtors are **accounted for** in a comprehensive illustrative example (involving settlement discounts). Folio numbers are shown in the accounts to illustrate the cross-referencing that is needed and in the example folio numbers begin with either:

(a)   SDB, referring to a page in the sales day book; or
(b)   SL, referring to a particular account in the sales ledger; or
(c)   ML, referring to a particular account in the main ledger; or
(d)   CB, referring to a page in the cash book.

Sales returns are shown as negative items in the SDB

At 1 July 20X7, the Software Design Company had no debtors at all. During July, the following transactions affecting credit sales and customers occurred. All sales figures are gross; VAT on sales is charged at 17.5%.

- July 3   Invoiced A Ashton for the sale on credit of hardware goods: £100.
- July 11   Invoiced B Bolton for the sale on credit of electrical goods: £150.
- July 15   Invoiced C Collins for the sale on credit of hardware goods: £250.
- July 17   Invoiced D Derby for the sale on credit of hardware goods: £400. Goods invoiced at £120 were returned for full credit on the next day.
- July 10   Received payment from A Ashton of £100, in settlement of his debt in full.
- July 18   Received a payment of £80 from B Bolton.
- July 28   Received a payment of £120 from C Collins.
- July 29   Received a payment of £280 from D Derby.

Cash sales in July amounted to £2,500, including VAT. Gross sales of £976 were for hardware goods, the balance for electrical.

Account numbers are as follows.

SL4   Personal account A Ashton
SL9   Personal account B Bolton
SL13 Personal account C Collins
SL21 Personal account D Derby
ML6   Sales ledger control account
ML21 Sales – hardware
ML22 Sales – electrical
ML1   Cash account
ML2   VAT account

113

The recording entries would be as follows.

SALES DAY BOOK
SDB35

Date	Name	Folio	Gross total £	VAT £	Net total £	Hard-ware £	Elect-rical £
20X7							
July 3	A Ashton	SL4 Dr	100.00	14.89	85.11	85.11	
July 11	B Bolton	SL9 Dr	150.00	22.34	127.66		127.66
July 15	C Collins	SL13 Dr	250.00	37.23	212.77	212.77	
July 17	D Derby	SL21 Dr	400.00	59.57	340.43	340.43	
July 18	D Derby	SL 21 Cr	(120.00)	(17.87)	(102.13)	(102.13)	
			780.00	116.16	663.84	536.18	127.66
			ML6 Dr	ML2 Cr		ML21 Cr	ML22 Cr

Note. The personal accounts in the sales ledger are debited on the day the invoices and credit notes are sent out. The double entry in the main ledger accounts might be made at the end of each day, week or month; here it is made at the end of the month, by posting from the sales day book as follows.

POSTING SUMMARY – SDB 35 31/7/X7

		Debit £	Credit £
ML 6	Sales ledger control account	780.00	
ML21	Sales – hardware		536.18
ML22	Sales – electrical		127.66
ML2	VAT		116.16

CASH BOOK EXTRACT
RECEIPTS – JULY 20X7
CB 23

Date	Name	Folio	Gross total £	VAT £	Net total £	Debtors £	Hard-ware £	Elect-rical £
20X7								
July 10	A Ashton	SL4 Cr	100.00			100.00		
July 18	B Bolton	SL9 Cr	80.00			80.00		
July 28	C Collins	SL13 Cr	120.00			120.00		
July 29	D Derby	SL 21 Cr	280.00			280.00		
July	Cash sales		2,500.00	372.34	2,127.66		830.64	1,297.02
			3,080.00	372.34	2,127.66	580.00	830.64	1,297.02
			ML1 Dr	ML2 Cr		ML 6 Cr	ML21 Cr	ML22 Cr

As with the sales day book, a posting summary to the main ledger needs to be drawn up for the cash book.

POSTING SUMMARY – CB 23 31/7/X7

		Debit £	Credit £
ML 1	Cash account	3,080.00	
ML 6	Sales ledger control account		580.00
ML 21	Sales – hardware		830.64
ML 22	Sales – electrical		1,297.02
ML 2	VAT		372.34

The personal accounts in the sales ledger are memorandum accounts, because they are not a part of the double entry system.

MEMORANDUM SALES LEDGER

A ASHTON — A/c no: SL4

Date 20X7	Narrative	Folio	£	Date 20X7	Narrative	Folio	£
July 3	Sales	SDB 35	100.00	July 10	Cash	CB 23	100.00
			100.00				100.00

B BOLTON — A/c no: SL9

Date 20X7	Narrative	Folio	£	Date 20X7	Narrative	Folio	£
July 11	Sales	SDB 35	150.00	July 18	Cash	CB 23	80.00
				July 31	Balance b/d		70.00
			150.00				150.00
Aug 1	Balance b/d		70.00				

C COLLINS — A/c no: SL13

Date 20X7	Narrative	Folio	£	Date 20X7	Narrative	Folio	£
July 15	Sales	SDB 35	250.00	July 28	Cash	CB 23	120.00
				July 31	Balance c/d		130.00
			250.00				250.00
Aug 1	Balance b/d		130.00				

D DERBY — A/c no: SL21

Date 20X7	Narrative	Folio	£	Date 20X7	Narrative	Folio	£
July 17	Sales	SDB 35	400.00	July 18	Returns	SDB 35	120.00
				July 29	Cash	CB 23	280.00
			400.00				400.00

In the main ledger, the accounting entries can be made from the books of prime entry to the ledger accounts, in this example at the end of the month.

MAIN LEDGER (EXTRACT)

SALES LEDGER CONTROL ACCOUNT (SLCA) A/c no: ML6

Date 20X7	Narrative	Folio	£	Date 20X7	Narrative	Folio	£
July 31	Sales	SDB 35	780.00	July 31	Cash	CB 23	580.00
					Balance c/d		200.00
			780.00				780.00
Aug 1	Balance b/d		200.00				

Note. At 31 July the closing balance on the sales ledger control account (£200) is the same as the total of the individual balances on the personal accounts in the sales ledger (£0 + £70 + £130 + £0).

VAT A/c no: ML 2

Date 20X7	Narrative	Folio	£	Date 20X7	Narrative	Folio	£
				July 31	SLCA	SDB 35	116.16
				July 31	Cash	CB 23	372.34

CASH ACCOUNT A/c no: ML1

Date 20X7	Narrative	Folio	£	Date	Narrative	Folio	£
July 31	Cash received	CB 23	3,080.00				

SALES – HARDWARE A/c no: ML21

Date	Narrative	Folio	£	Date 20X7	Narrative	Folio	£
				July 31	SLCA	SDB 35	536.18
				July 31	Cash	CB 23	830.64

SALES – ELECTRICAL A/c no: ML22

Date	Narrative	Folio	£	Date 20X7	Narrative	Folio	£
				July 31	SLCA	SDB 35	127.66
				July 31	Cash	CB 23	1,297.02

If we took the balance on the accounts shown in this example as at 31 July 20X7 the list of balances would be as follows.

TRIAL BALANCE 31/7/X7

	Debit £	Credit £
Cash (all receipts)	3,080.00	
Sales ledger control account	200.00	
VAT		488.50
Sales – hardware		1,366.82
Sales – electrical		1,424.68
	3,280.00	3,280.00

This must **include** the balances on control accounts, but **exclude** the balances on the personal accounts in the sales ledger, which are **memorandum** accounts.

Activity 6.3

Ali informs you that the following information for the year ended 31 May 20X7 comes from the accounting records of Joanne Smith.

	£
Sales ledger control account as at 1 June 20X6	
Debit balance	12,404.86
Credit balance	322.94
Credit sales	96,464.41
Goods returned from trade debtors	1,142.92
Payments received from trade debtors	94,648.71*
Discounts allowed to trade debtors	3,311.47**

* This figures includes cheques totalling £192.00 which were dishonoured before 31 May 20X7, the debts in respect of which remained outstanding at 31 May 20X7. The only sales ledger account with a credit balance at 31 May 20X7 was that of ENR Ltd with a balance of £337.75.

** The discounts are all settlement discounts, taken against invoice values.

You are told that, after the preparation of the sales ledger control account for the year ended 31 May 20X7 from the information given above, the following accounting errors were discovered.

(i) In July 20X7, a debt due of £77.00 from PAL Ltd had been written off as bad. Whilst the correct entries have been made in PAL Ltd's personal account, no reference to the debt being written off has been made in the sales ledger control account.

(ii) Cash sales of £3,440.00 in November 20X6 have been included in the payments received from trade debtors of £94,648.71.

(iii) The sales day book for January 20X7 had been undercast by £427.80.

(iv) Credit sales £96,464.41 includes goods costing £3,711.86 returned to suppliers by Joanne.

(v) No entries have been made in the personal accounts for goods returned from trade debtors of £1,142.92.

(vi) The debit side of FTR Ltd's personal account has been overcast by £71.66.

Tasks

(a) Prepare the sales ledger control account for the year ended 31 May 20X7 as it would have been *before* the various accounting errors outlined above were discovered.

(b) Prepare an adjusted control account showing trade debtors as at 31 May 20X7.

Tutorial note. Think carefully whether all the errors listed affect the control account.

6 Purpose of the sales ledger control account

There are a number of reasons for having a sales ledger control account, mainly to do with the usefulness of **reconciling the control account to the list of memorandum sales ledger balances.**

Purpose	Details
To check the accuracy of entries made in the personal accounts	Comparing the balance on the sales ledger control account with the total of individual balances on the sales ledger personal accounts means we can identify the fact that errors have been made.
To **trace errors**	By using the sales ledger control account, a comparison with the individual balances in the sales ledger can be made for **every week** or **day** of the month, and the error found much more quickly than if a control account like this did not exist.
To provide an **internal check**	The person posting entries to the sales ledger control account will act as a check on a different person whose job it is to post entries to the sales ledger accounts.
To provide a **debtors balance quickly**	This is useful when producing a trial balance.

7 Sales ledger control account reconciliation

The sales ledger control account should be **balanced regularly** (at least monthly), and the balance on the account **agreed to the sum of the individual debtors' balances** extracted from the sales ledger.

In practice, more often than not the balance on the control account does not agree with the sum of balances extracted, for one or more of the following reasons.

Reason for disagreement	How to correct
Miscast of the total in the book of prime entry (adding up incorrectly).	The main ledger debit and credit postings will balance, but the sales ledger control account balance will not agree with the sum of individual balances extracted from the (memorandum) sales ledger. A journal entry must then be made in the main ledger to correct the sales ledger control account and the corresponding sales account.
A **transposition error** in **posting** an individual's transaction from the book of prime entry to the memorandum ledger.	For example the sale to C Collins of £250 might be posted to his account as £520. The **sum of balances** extracted from the memorandum ledger **must be corrected**. No accounting entry would be required to do this, except to alter the figure in C Collins' account.
Omission of a transaction from the sales ledger control account or the memorandum account, but not both.	A single entry will correct an omission from the memorandum account in the sales ledger. Where a transaction is missing from the sales ledger control account, then the double entry will have to be checked and corrected.

Reason for disagreement	How to correct
The **sum of balances** extracted from the sales ledger may be **incorrectly extracted** or **miscast**.	Correct the total of the balances.

Reconciling the sales ledger control account balance with the sum of the balances extracted from the (memorandum) sales ledger is an important procedure. It should be performed **regularly** so that any errors are revealed and appropriate action can be taken. The reconciliation should be done in five steps.

Step 1 Balance the accounts in the memorandum ledger, and review for errors.

Step 2 Correct the total of the balances extracted from the memorandum ledger.

	£	£
Sales ledger total		
Original total extracted		15,320
Add: difference arising from transposition error		
(£95 written as £59)		36
		15,356
Less: Credit balance of £60 extracted as a debit balance		
(£60 × 2)	120	
Overcast of list of balances	90	
		(210)
		15,146

Step 3 Balance the sales ledger control account, and review for errors.

Step 4 Adjust or post the sales ledger control account **with correcting entries.**

Step 5 Prepare a statement showing how the corrected sales ledger agrees to the corrected sales ledger control account.

SALES LEDGER CONTROL ACCOUNT

	£		£
Balance before adjustments	15,091	Returns inwards: individual posting omitted from control a/c	45
		Balance c/d	15,146
Undercast of total invoices issued in sales day book	100	(now in agreement with the corrected total of individual balances above)	
	15,191		15,191
Balance b/d	15,146		

Once the five steps are completed, the total sales ledger balances should equal the sales ledger control account balance.

The sales ledger control account reconciliation will be carried out by the **sales ledger clerk** and reviewed and approved by a **senior member of staff**.

Activity 6.4

(a) You are employed by Joanne and have been asked to help prepare the end of year accounts for the period ended 31 May 20X8 by agreeing the figure for total debtors.

The following figures, relating to the financial year, have been obtained from the books of prime entry.

	£
Purchases for the year	361,947
Sales	472,185
Returns inwards	41,226
Returns outwards	16,979
Bad debts written off	1,914
Discounts allowed	2,672
Discounts received	1,864
Cheques paid to creditors	342,791
Cheques received from debtors	429,811
Customer cheques dishonoured	626

You discover that at the close of business on 31 May 20X7 the total of the debtors amounted to £50,241.

Task

Prepare Joanne's sales ledger control account for the year ended 31 May 20X8.

(b) To give you some assistance, your rather inexperienced colleague, Peter Johnson, has attempted to extract and total the individual balances in the sales ledger. He provides you with the following listing which he has prepared.

	£
Bury plc	7,500
P Fox & Son (Swindon) Ltd	2,000
Frank Wendlebury & Co Ltd	4,297
D Richardson & Co Ltd	6,847
Ultra Ltd	783
Lawrenson Ltd	3,765
Walkers plc	4,091
P Fox & Son (Swindon) Ltd	2,000
Whitchurch Ltd	8,112
Ron Bradbury & Co Ltd	5,910
Anderson Ltd	1,442
	46,347

Subsequent to the drawing up of the list, the following errors have so far been found.

(i) A sales invoice for £267 sent to Whitchurch Ltd had been correctly entered in the day book but had not then been posted to the account for Whitchurch Ltd in the sales ledger.

(ii) One of the errors made by Peter Johnson (you suspect that his list may contain others) was to omit the £2,435 balance of Rectofon Ltd from the list.

(iii) A credit note for £95 sent to Bury plc had been correctly entered in the day book but was entered in the account in the sales ledger as £75.

Task

Prepare a statement reconciling the £46,347 total provided by Peter Johnson with the balance of your own sales ledger control account.

Key learning points

☑ A control account is an account which **keeps a total record for a collective item** (for example debtors) which in reality consists of many individual items (for example individual debtors). It is an impersonal account maintained in the main ledger.

☑ The **sales ledger control account** is a **record of the total of the balances owed by customers**. Postings are made from the sales and sales returns day books, the cash book and the journal, in order to maintain this record.

☑ The **sales ledger control account serves a number of purposes.**

– It provides a check on the accuracy of entries made in the personal sales ledger accounts, and helps with the tracing of any errors which may have occurred.

– It also provides an internal check on employees' work.

– It gives a convenient total debtors balance when the time comes to produce a trial balance or a balance sheet.

☑ The **balance on the sales ledger control account** should be **reconciled regularly with the sum of the memorandum sales ledger account balances** so that any necessary action can be taken.

Quick quiz

1   What is a control account?

2   What does the balance on the sales ledger control account represent?

3   A dishonoured cheque is a credit entry in the sales ledger control account. True or false?

4   How might a credit balance arise in the sales ledger control account?

5   What is a trial balance?

6   Why might the balance on the sales ledger control account not agree with the total of the individual debtors' balances?

Answers to quick quiz

1   An account in which a record is kept of the total value of a number of similar but individual items.

2   The total amount due to the business from its debtors.

3   False. Cash received is a credit entry, therefore a dishonoured cheque must be a debit.

4   A customer may return goods or overpay his balance.

5   A list of all the balances in the main ledger at any one time.

6   (i)   There may be a transposition error in posting an individual's transaction from the book of prime entry to the memorandum ledger.

    (ii)   The day book could be miscast.

    (iii) A transaction may be omitted from the control account or the memorandum account.

    (iv)   The list of balances may be incorrectly extracted.

chapter 7

Purchase ledger control account

Contents

1 The problem

As we had problems seeing how the double entry system worked for debtors, we have the same problem **with creditors**.

2 The solution

As we saw in Chapter 6 for debtors, the double entry is solved by using a **control account**, the **purchase ledger control account**.

3 Purpose of the purchase ledger control account

The balance on the purchase ledger control account at any time will be the **total amount owed by the business at that time to its creditors.**

The purchase ledger control account records all of the transactions involving the creditors of the business.

The purchase ledger control account, like the sales ledger control account, provides:

- A check on the **accuracy of entries** in the individual personal accounts
- Help in **locating errors**
- A form of **internal check**
- A total trade creditors' balance for when a **trial balance** or balance sheet needs to be prepared

3.1 How the control account works

It works very much like the sales ledger control account.

Step 1	The **purchase day book** records the individual purchase invoices and credit notes which a business receives (unless there is also a purchase returns day book).
Step 2	Each transaction is recorded individually in the appropriate personal account in the **purchase ledger** for the supplier from whom the invoice or credit note has been received.
Step 3	The personal accounts for creditors are, in many accounting systems, **memorandum accounts** and do not as such form a part of the double entry system of accounting.
Step 4	The total purchase invoice and credit note transactions shown in the day books can be posted to the main ledger using **double entry.**

Activity 7.1

Which one of the following statements describes the relationship between the **purchase ledger control account and the purchase ledger?**

A   The **purchase ledger control account** is where the corresponding debit side of credit entries to the **purchase ledger** are posted.

B   The **purchase ledger control account** is where invoices from customers for whom you have not set up an account in the **purchase ledger** are posted.

C   The **purchase ledger** is a memorandum list of invoices and related transactions analysed by customer. The **purchase ledger control account** is the total of creditor balances, and is in the balance sheet.

D   The **purchase ledger** forms part of the double entry. The **purchase ledger control account** is a memorandum control total used for internal checking purposes.

4 Posting to the purchase ledger control account

Typical entries in the purchase ledger control account are shown in the example below. The references PDB and PRDB are to the purchase day book and purchase returns day book respectively.

PURCHASE LEDGER CONTROL ACCOUNT (PLCA)

	Folio	£		Folio	£
Opening debit balances	b/d	70	Opening credit balances	b/d	8,300
Cash paid	CB	29,840	Purchases and other		
Discounts received	CB	30	expenses	PDB	31,000
Returns outwards	PRDB	60	Cash received clearing		
Closing credit balances	c/d	9,400	debit balances	CB	20
			Closing debit balances	c/d	80
		39,400			39,400
Debit balances	b/d	80	Credit balances	b/d	9,400

Let's consider these ent in more detail.

Debit entries	Double entry
Opening debit balances	This is unusual, perhaps an overpayment to a creditor, or a payment made before a supplier has sent an invoice.
Cash paid	Reduces a liability, therefore a **debit** (**credit** cash).
Discounts received	The debit is the difference between the full amount invoiced by suppliers and the discounted amount which we paid. **Debit** PLCA **credit** discounts received.

Debit entries	Double entry
Returns outwards	These are returns of goods to suppliers recorded as credit notes received. **Debit** PLCA, **credit** purchases.
Closing credit balances	Represent the **total** of the creditors carried down.
Credit entries	**Double entry**
Opening credit balances	Represent total creditors brought down (disregarding any debit balances).
Purchases and other expenses	The amounts invoiced by suppliers. **Debit** purchases, **credit** PLCA.
Cash received clearing debit balances	An unusual item. **Debit** cash, **credit** PLCA.
Closing debit balances	Carried down separately from credit balances.

Example: Control accounts

The following example involves both sales and purchase information. You must be able to distinguish relevant information for the task set.

On examining the books of Steps Ltd, you discover that on 1 October 20X1 the purchase ledger balances were £6,235 credit and £105 debit.

For the year ended 30 September 20X2 the following details are available.

	£
Sales	63,728
Purchases	39,974
Cash received from debtors	55,212
Cash paid to creditors	37,307
Discount received	1,475
Discount allowed	2,328
Returns inwards	1,002
Returns outwards	535
Bad debts written off	326
Cash received in respect of debit balances in purchase ledger	105
Amount due from customer as shown by sales ledger, offset against amount due to the same firm as shown by purchase ledger (settlement by contra)	434

On 30 September 20X2 there were no debit balances in the purchase ledger.

We need to write up the purchase ledger control account recording the above transactions and bringing down balances at 30 September 20X2.

Solution

PURCHASE LEDGER CONTROL ACCOUNT

20X1		£	20X1		£
Oct 1	Balances b/d	105	Oct 1	Balances b/d	6,235
20X2			20X2		
Sept 30	Cash paid to creditors	37,307	Sept 30	Purchases	39,974
	Discount received	1,475		Cash	105
	Returns outwards	535			
	Contra sales ledger				
	control account	434			
	Balances c/d	6,458			
		46,314			46,314

Tutorial note. As contra entries reduce the amounts outstanding, they will always be **debit** PLCA, **credit** SLCA.

5 Purchase ledger control account reconciliation

There are good reasons for performing this reconciliation.

(a)   The account should be **balanced regularly.**

(b)   The balance on the account should be agreed with the sum of the individual creditors' balances extracted from the purchase ledger.

As with the sales ledger control account, this routine will be carried out on a monthly basis in many businesses.

Items in the reconciliation are likely to arise from similar occurrences to those already identified in the case of the sales ledger control account discussed in Chapter 6.

Error	Affects
• Miscast of purchase day book or cash book	Purchase ledger control account
• Transposition error in entry from day book to purchase ledger	Purchase ledger balances
• Missing entries in *either* purchase ledger *or* control account	*Either* purchase ledger *or* control account
• Miscast of total purchase ledger balances	Purchase ledger balances
• Miscast of purchase ledger control account	Purchase ledger control account

The reconciliation of the purchase ledger control account should be carried out in five steps.

Step 1	Balance the accounts in the memorandum purchase ledger, and review for errors.
Step 2	Correct the total of the balances extracted from the memorandum purchase ledger.
Step 3	Balance the purchase ledger control account, and review for errors.
Step 4	Adjust or post the necessary correcting entries to the account.
Step 5	Prepare a statement showing how the corrected purchase ledger agrees to the corrected purchase ledger control account.

In the example below, it is necessary to write up the account for the year and then to prepare the **control account reconciliation statement**.

Example: Control account reconciliation

Minster plc at present makes use of a manual system of accounting consisting of a main ledger, a sales ledger and a purchase ledger together with books of prime entry. The various accounts within the ledgers are drawn up on ledger cards which are updated by hand from the books of prime entry when relevant transactions take place. The decision has now been taken to use a control account in the main ledger to help keep a check on the purchase ledger and the following figures relating to the financial year ended 31 October 20X1 have been extracted from the books of prime entry.

	£
Credit purchases	132,485
Cash purchases	18,917
Credit notes received from credit suppliers	2,361
Discounts received from credit suppliers	4,153
Cheques paid to credit suppliers	124,426
Balances in the sales ledger set off against balances in the purchase ledger	542

On 1 November 20X0 the total of the creditors was £28,603.

The purchase ledger accounts have been totalled at £28,185 as at 31 October 20X1.

Subsequent to the totalling procedure, the following matters are discovered.

(a) Whilst the totalling was taking place, the chief accountant was reviewing the account of Peterbury Ltd, a supplier, and the ledger card was on his desk. The balance of the account at 31 October was £1,836.

(b) A credit note for £387 issued by John Danbury Ltd, a credit supplier, was correctly entered in the day book but had not then been posted to John Danbury Ltd's account in the ledger.

(c) An invoice for £1,204 issued by Hartley Ltd, a credit supplier, was correctly entered in the day book and was then entered in Hardy Ltd's account in the purchase ledger.

(d) An invoice for £898 relating to a credit purchase from Intergram plc, although correctly entered in the day book, was posted to the supplier's account in the ledger as £889.

(e) A discount for £37 allowed to Minster plc by the credit supplier K Barden Ltd, had been correctly entered in the cash book but was then omitted from the company's account in the ledger.

Tasks

(a)   Prepare Minster plc's creditors control account for the year ended 31 October 20X1.

(b)   Prepare a statement reconciling the original total of the purchase ledger accounts with the balance of your creditors control account.

Solution

(a)

PURCHASE LEDGER CONTROL ACCOUNT

	£		£
Credit notes received	2,361	Balance b/d	28,603
Discounts received	4,153	Purchases	132,485
Bank	124,426		
Contra sales ledger	542		
Balance c/d	29,606		
	161,088		161,088

(b)

	£	£
Balance as per listing of creditors' accounts		28,185
Add:		
Peterbury Ltd ledger card omitted	1,836	
Posting error (Intergram plc)	9	
		1,845
		30,030
Less:		
Credit note not posted	387	
Discount received (K Barden Ltd)	37	
		424
Balance as per purchase ledger control account		29,606

Note. Item (c), the invoice from Hartley Ltd, although entered in the wrong personal account, is included in the purchase ledger listing and so does not affect the total.

Activity 7.2

(a)   Which, if any, of the following could you see in a reconciliation of the purchase ledger control account with the purchase ledger list of balances?

    (i)   Mispostings of cash payments to suppliers
    (ii)   Casting errors
    (iii)   Transposition errors

(b)   Which of the following would you not expect to see reflected in a *purchase ledger control account*?

       (i)   Dividend payments
       (ii)   Invoices received, in summary
       (iii)   Drawings
       (iv)   Cheque payments
       (v)   Contras
       (vi)   Returns to suppliers
       (vii)   Debit notes to suppliers
       (viii) Discounts received

(c)   You would never see a debit balance on a purchase ledger account.

	Tick
True	☐
False	☐

Activity 7.3

A computerised accounting system contains three modules:

(a)   Main ledger
(b)   Purchase ledger
(c)   Sales ledger

The system is an integrated one. This means that postings to the main ledger are made automatically from the sales and purchase ledgers.

In this situation, indicate whether the following statement is TRUE or FALSE.

		Tick
The creditors control account total will *always* agree with the sum of the balances on the individual creditor accounts in the purchase ledger, and no disagreement is ever possible	True	☐
	False	☐

Activity 7.4

You are employed by Joanne Smith. You have ascertained that as at 31 May 20X7 the purchase ledger control account balance of £57,997.34 does not agree with the total of the balances extracted from the purchase ledger of £54,842.40.

On investigation, some errors come to light.

(i)   An account with a balance of £8,300.00 had been omitted from the purchase ledger balances.

(ii)   Purchases of £7,449.60 for April had not been credited to the purchase ledger control account.

(iii)   RNH Ltd's account in the purchase ledger had been undercast by £620.40.

(iv)   A van bought on credit for £6,400.00 had been credited to the purchase ledger control account.

(v)   Returns outwards of £1,424.50 had been omitted from the purchase ledger control account.

(vi)   A cheque for £5,000.00 payable to SPL Ltd had not been debited to its account in the purchase ledger.

(vii) Discounts received of £740.36 had been entered twice in the purchase ledger control account.

(viii) A contra arrangement of £400.00 with a trade debtor had not been set off in the purchase ledger.

Helping hand. With item (vi), think carefully whether you are adding or deducting.

Task

Set out the necessary adjustments to:

(a)   The schedule of balances as extracted from the purchase ledger

(b)   The balance in the purchase ledger control account

And finally ...

Look back to the diagram in Section 3 of Chapter 2. Now you know about control accounts, it will all fall into place!

Key learning points

☑ The **purchase ledger control account (PLCA)** records the true total of the balances owed to credit suppliers. This record is prepared from postings from the purchase and purchase returns day books, the cash book and the journal.

☑ The PLCA **acts as a check on the accuracy of individual suppliers' accounts** in the purchase ledger, as well as acting as a **form of internal check**. If a trial balance or balance sheet is needed, a total trade creditors' balance can be extracted from the account.

☑ The **balance on the PLCA should be reconciled regularly with the sum of the memorandum purchase ledger account balances.**

Quick quiz

1   What does the balance on the purchase ledger control account represent?

2   Name two uses of a purchase ledger control account.

3   Discounts received from suppliers are credited to the purchase ledger control account. True or false?

4   What is the double entry for cash received to clear a debit balance on the purchase ledger control account?

5   The purchase day book is miscast. Would this affect the purchase ledger control account or the purchase ledger?

6   An invoice has been incorrectly entered in the purchase day book. Would this give rise to a difference between the purchase ledger control account and the total of purchase ledger balances?

Answers to quick quiz

1   The total amount owed by the business to its creditors.

2   (i)   Checks accuracy of entries in the personal accounts.
    (ii) Provides a total creditors figure for the list of balances.

3   False. They reduce the liability, so they are debited.

4   DEBIT   Cash
    CREDIT   Purchase ledger control account

5   The purchase ledger control account.

6   No. Both would be incorrect.

chapter 8

Bank

reconciliations

Contents

1 The problem

By now you'll be familiar with the cash book. But this is a record of the amount of cash the business **thinks** it has in the bank.

You, too, may have an idea of what your bank balance should be. But then you get your bank statement, and the amount is rather different...

2 The solution

A bank reconciliation compares entries in the cash book and the bank statement and identifies differences.

3 Bank reconciliations

3.1 Why is a bank reconciliation necessary?

Why might your own estimate of your bank balance be different from the amount shown on your bank statement? There are three common explanations.

Cause of difference	Explanation
Errors	Errors in calculation, or in recording income and payments, are as likely to have been made by yourself as the bank. These **errors must be corrected**.
Bank charges or bank interest	The bank might deduct interest on an overdraft or charges for its services, which you are not informed about until you receive the bank statement. **These should be accounted for in your records**.
Timing differences	(a) **Cheques recorded as received** and paid-in but not yet 'cleared' and added to your account by the bank. This will be resolved in a very short time when the cheques are eventually cleared. (b) **Payments made by cheque** and recorded, but not yet banked by the payee. Even when they are banked, it takes a day or two for the banks to process them and for the money to be deducted from your account. These are known as **unpresented cheques**.

4 The bank statement

It is common practice for a bank to issue a monthly **statement** to each customer, itemising:

- The **balance** on the account **at the beginning** of the month
- Deposits and receipts due to the customer during the month
- **Payments** made by the customer during the month
- The **balance** the customer has on his account **at the end of the month**

> **REMEMBER!**
>
> If you have money in your account, **the bank owes you that money**, and you are a **creditor** of the bank. (If you are in 'credit', you have money in your bank account.)
>
> However, in your books of account, if you have money in your account it is an asset (a **debit** balance) and the bank owes you that money (is your **debtor**).

If a business has £8,000 in the bank. It will have a debit balance in its own cash book, but the bank statement will show a credit balance of £8,000.

The bank's records are a 'mirror image' of the customer's own records, with debits and credits reversed. It is similar to a supplier's statement, which records the supplier's sales but the customer's purchases.

4.1 What does a bank statement look like?

An example of a bank statement is shown below; nearly all bank statements will look something like this.

Southern Bank   CONFIDENTIAL

200 BROMFORD AVENUE	Account ABC & CO	SHEET NO 52
LONDON	4 THE MEWS	(d)
E11 8TH	LONDON E4 2P2	

Telephone

20X2   020 8359 3100   Statement date   13 JUN 20X2 (a)   Account no   9309823 (b)

Date	Details	Withdrawals	Deposits	Balance (£)
(c) 11MAY	Balance from Sheet no. 51 (d)			(f) 787.58
14MAY	000059 (g)	216.81		570.77
22MAY	000058	157.37		413.40
24MAY	000060	22.00		391.40
29MAY	LION INSURANCE DD (i)	87.32		
	CATS238/ 948392093 DD	1,140.10		
	LB HACKBETH CC SO (j)	54.69		
	COUNTER CREDIT 101479 (h)		469.86	
	INTEREST (l)	9.32		
	CHARGES (k)	30.00		460.17 O'D
13JUN	Balance to Sheet no. 53			(f) 460.17 O'D

(e) **Key** **SO** Standing Order **DV** Dividend **CC** Cash &/or Cheques   Auto Withdrawals **AC** Automated cash **PY** Payroll   **Interest -** see over
EC Eurocheque **TR** Transfer **CP** Card Purchases   **DD** Direct Debit **OD** Overdrawn

Letter	Item	Explanation
(a)	Statement date	Only transactions which have passed through your account **up to this date** (and since the last statement date) will be shown on the statement.
(b)	Account number	This number is required on the statement, particularly if the bank's customer has **more than one account**.
(c)	Date	This shows the date any transaction **cleared** into or out of your account. You may have made the transaction earlier.
(d)	Sheet number	Each bank statement received will have a number. The numbers run in **sequential order**; this shows if a statement is missing.
(e)	Key	Not all bank statements will have a key to the abbreviations they use but it is helpful when one is provided. Note the following. • **Dividends** can be paid directly into a bank account. • **Automated cash** is a withdrawal from an automated teller machine - unusual for a business. • **Card purchase** is a purchase by debit card, again unusual for a business.
(f)	Balance	Most statements show a balance as at the end of each day's transactions.
(g)	Cheque numbers	The number is the same as that which appears on the individual cheque. Numbers are necessary to help you to **identify items** on the statement: you could not do so if only the amount of the cheque appeared.
(h)	Paying-in slip numbers	The need for these numbers is the same as for cheques.
(i)	Direct debit payments and receipts	The **recipient** of the direct debit payment is usually identified, either in words or by an account number.
(j)	Standing order payments and receipts	Again, the recipient is identifiable.
(k)	Charges	Based on the **number of transactions** (cheques, receipts and so on) which have been processed through your account in a given period (usually a quarter).
(l)	Interest	Interest is charged on the amount of an **overdrawn balance** for the period it is overdrawn.

Activity 8.1

The bank statement of Joanne Smith for the month of February 20X7 is shown below.

Task

You are required to explain briefly the shaded items on the statement.

Southern Bank

CONFIDENTIAL

Clapham Common Branch
Clapham Common
London SW6

Account   Joanne Smith
3 Barnes Street
Clapham SW6

SHEET NO   72

Telephone   020 7728 4213

20X7   Statement date   28 February 20X7   Account no   01140146

Date	Details		Withdrawals	Deposits	Balance (£)
	Balance brought forward				1,225.37
1 Feb	Cheque	800120	420.00		805.37
4 Feb	Cheque	800119	135.40		669.97
7 Feb	Bank giro credit	Pronto Motors		162.40	
7 Feb	Credit			380.75	
7 Feb	BACS	7492	124.20		1,088.92
9 Feb	Cheque	800121	824.70		264.22
11 Feb	Cheque	800122	323.25		59.03 OD
14 Feb	Credit			522.70	463.67
19 Feb	Credit			122.08	585.75
21 Feb	BACS		124.20		
21 Feb	Direct debit	Swingate Ltd	121.00		340.55
23 Feb	Bank giro credit	Bord & Sons		194.60	535.15
25 Feb	Cheque	800123	150.00		385.15
27 Feb	Credit			242.18	627.33
28 Feb	Bank charges		15.40		611.93
28 Feb	Balance to Sheet no.	73			611.93

5 How to perform a bank reconciliation

5.1 The reconciliation

The **cash book and bank statement will rarely agree at a given date**. Several procedures should be followed to ensure that the reconciliation between them is performed correctly.

Step 1	Identify the cash book balance and the bank balance (from the bank statement) on the date to which you wish to reconcile.
Step 2	Add up the cash book for the period since the last reconciliation and identify and note any errors found.
Step 3	Examine the bank statements for the same period and identify those items which appear on the bank statement but which have not been entered in the cash book.

- Standing orders and direct debits (into and out of the account)
- Dividend receipts from investments
- Bank charges and interest

Make a list of all those found.

Step 4	Identify all reconciling items due to timing differences.

(a) Some cheque payments entered in the cash book have not yet been presented to the bank, or 'cleared', and so do not yet appear on the bank statement.

(b) Cheques received, entered in the cash book and paid into the bank, but which have not yet been cleared and entered in the account by the bank, do not yet appear on the bank statement.

5.2 What does a bank reconciliation look like?

ADJUSTED CASH BOOK BALANCE

	£	£
Cash book balance brought down		X
Add: correction of understatement	X	
receipts not entered in cash book (standing orders, direct debits)	X̲	
		X
Less: correction of overstatement	X	
payments/charges not entered in cash book (standing orders, direct debits)	X̲	
		(X̲)
Corrected cash book balance		A̲

BANK RECONCILIATION	£
Balance per bank statement	X
Add: cheques paid in and recorded in the cash book but not yet credited to the account by the bank (**outstanding lodgements**)	X
Less: cheques paid by the business but not yet presented to the business's bank for settlement (**unpresented cheques**)	(X̲)
Balance per cash book	A̲

Example: Bank reconciliation

At 30 September 20X3 the debit balance in the cash book of Dotcom Ltd was £805.15. A bank statement on 30 September 20X3 showed Dotcom Ltd to be in credit by £1,112.30.

On investigation of the difference between the two sums, three things come to light.

(a) The cash book had been added up wrongly on the debit side; it should have been £90.00 more.
(b) Cheques paid in but not yet credited by the bank amounted to £208.20.
(c) Cheques drawn but not yet presented to the bank amounted to £425.35.

We need to show the correction to the cash book and show a statement reconciling the balance per the bank statement to the balance in the cash book.

Solution

BANK RECONCILIATION 30.9.X3

	£	£
Cash book balance brought down		805.15
Add: correction of adding-up		90.00
Corrected balance		895.15
Balance per bank statement		1,112.30
Add: cheques paid in, recorded in the cash book, but		
not yet credited to the account by the bank	208.20	
Less: cheques paid by the company but not yet presented		
to the company's bank for settlement	(425.35)	
		(217.15)
Balance per cash book		895.15

The reconciling items noted here will often consist of several transactions which can either be listed on the face of the reconciliation or listed separately. In particular, there may be a **great many outstanding cheques** if this is a busy business account.

You can see here that the reconciliation falls into **two distinct steps**:

> **Step 1**   Correct the cash book.
>
> **Step 2**   Reconcile the bank balance to the corrected cash book balance.

Activity 8.2

The cash book of Joanne Smith for February 20X7 is set out below.

CASH BOOK

Receipts			Payments			
Date	Details		Date	Details	Cheq no	
20X7		£	20X7			£
1/2	Balance b/d	1,089.97	1/2	Rent	800120	420.00
3/2	Pronto Motors	162.40	4/2	R F Lessing	800121	824.70
3/2	Cash sales	380.75	4/2	Wages	BACS	124.20
11/2	Cash sales	522.70	11/2	British Gas plc	800122	323.25
16/2	Cash sales	122.08	18/2	D Waite	800123	150.00
24/2	Cash sales	242.18	18/2	Wages	BACS	124.20
28/2	Warley's Ltd	342.50	23/2	S Molesworth	800124	207.05
			25/2	Fogwell & Co	800125	92.44
			28/2	Balance c/d		596.74
		2,862.58				2,862.58
	Balance b/d	596.74				

Task

Using the information from the bank statement (Activity 8.1), complete the cash book entries for the month. (The transactions to be entered are those which appear on the bank statement but are not to be found in the cash book as shown above.) You do not need to reproduce the whole of the cash book given above. Use the balance b/d figure as your starting point.

The following additional information is available. The difference between the opening bank balance at 1 February per the cash book of £1,089.97 and the opening balance at 1 February per the bank statement of £1,225.37 CR is explained by the cheque number 800119 for £135.40 which was recorded in the cash book in January and presented on 7 February.

Activity 8.3

Prepare a bank reconciliation statement for Joanne Smith as at 28 February 20X7 using the information given in Activities 8.1 and 8.2.

5.3 Timing and frequency of the bank reconciliation

When and how often a business's bank reconciliation is performed depends on several factors.

Factor	Considerations
Frequency and volume of transactions	The more transactions there are, then the greater the likelihood of error.
Other controls	If there are very few checks on cash other than the reconciliation, then it should be performed quite often. (Other checks would include agreeing receipts to remittance advices.)
Cash flow	If the business has to keep a very close watch on its cash position then the reconciliation should be performed as often as the information on cash balances is required. Most businesses do a reconciliation at the end of each month. If a business is very close to its overdraft limit, then it might need to do a weekly reconciliation.
Number of bank accounts	If, for some reason, a business has several bank accounts, all used regularly, then it may be impractical, or even impossible, to perform reconciliations very often.

Activity 8.4

At your firm, Gemfix Engineering Ltd, a new trainee has been asked to prepare a bank reconciliation statement as at the end of October 20X7. At 31 October 20X7, the company's bank statement shows an overdrawn balance of £142.50 DR and the cash book shows a favourable balance of £24.13.

You are concerned that the trainee has been asked to prepare the statement without proper training for the task. The trainee prepares the schedule below and asks you to look over it.

	£
Balance per bank statement (overdrawn)	142.50
Overdraft interest on bank statement, not in cash book	24.88
Unpresented cheques (total)	121.25
Cheque paid in, not credited on bank statement	(290.00)
Error in cash book*	27.00
	25.63
Unexplained difference	(1.50)
Balance per cash book	24.13

*Cheque issued for £136.00, shown as £163.00 in the cash book.

The trainee says that he was not able to reconcile the difference completely, but was pleased that he was able to 'get it down' to £1.50. He feels that there is no need to do any more work now since the difference remaining is so small. He suggests leaving the job on one side for a week or so in the hope that the necessary information will come to light during that period.

Tasks

(a)   So that you can show the trainee how a bank reconciliation ought to be performed, prepare:

(i)   A statement of adjustments to be made to the cash book balance

(ii)   A corrected bank reconciliation statement as at 31 October 20X7

(b)   Explain to the trainee why it is important to prepare bank reconciliations regularly and on time.

5.4 Stopped cheques

When you have received a cheque and banked it but it has already been stopped by the drawer, then the bank will not process it.

(a)   You have already written the receipt in your cash book, but now it must be taken out again.

(b)   This can be shown in the cash book as a deduction from receipts or an addition to payments, whichever is easier.

If you have written a cheque to someone and then subsequently you stop it, you must remove the payment from the cash book. If the reversal of the entry is not carried out then it will appear as a reconciling item on the bank reconciliation.

5.5 Out of date cheques

Banks consider cheques 'stale' after six months. Cheques which have been written but which have not been presented to the bank will continue to appear on a reconciliation month after month.

Step 1	Every time the reconciliation is performed you should check whether the oldest outstanding cheques are over six months old.
Step 2	Cancel or 'write back' such cheques in the cash book; they will then cease to be reconciling items.
Step 3	Notify the bank to stop the cheque as a precaution.
Step 4	Raise a new cheque.

5.6 Standing orders and direct debit schedule

Never just accept that a standing order or direct debit appearing on the bank statement is correct. The organisation must keep an up to date schedule of all current standing orders and direct debit.

Whenever a bank reconciliation is carried out, you must check all payments and/or receipts under standing order or direct debit to this schedule.

*   The bank may use the wrong amount, particularly if the order or debit has been changed recently.
*   The bank may pay an order or debit that has been recently cancelled.
*   The bank may miss an order or debit that has been recently set up.
*   The business may need to cancel an order or debit that has been overlooked.

Activity 8.5

On 1 October 20X0, Talbot Windows received a bank statement for the month of September 20X0.

(a)   Update the cash book, checking items against the bank statement. Total the cash book, showing clearly the balance carried down.

(b)   Prepare a reconciliation statement.

WEST BANK plc

220 High Street, Bolton, BL9 4BQ

To: Talbot Windows   Account No 48104039   30 September 20X0

STATEMENT OF ACCOUNT

DATE	DETAILS	DEBIT	CREDIT	BALANCE
20X0		£	£	£
1 Sept	Balance b/f			13,400
4 Sept	Cheque No 108300	1,200		12,200
1 Sept	Counter credit		400	12,600
8 Sept	Credit transfer			
	Zebra Sales		4,000	16,600
10 Sept	Cheque No 108301	470		16,130
16 Sept	Standing order			
	West Council	300		15,830
24 Sept	Bank charges	132		15,698
25 Sept	Standing order			
	Any Bank	400		15,298
30 Sept	Cheque No 108303	160		15,138
30 Sept	Credit transfer			
	Bristol Ltd		2,000	17,138
30 Sept	Salaries	9,024		8,114

CASH BOOK

Date	Details	Bank	Date	Cheque	Details	Bank
20X0		£	20X0	No		£
1 Sept	Balance b/f	13,400	1 Sept	108300	J Hibbert	1,200
1 Sept	L Peters	400	5 Sept	108301	Cleanglass	470
28 Sept	John Smith	2,400	25 Sept	108302	Denham Insurers	630
29 Sept	KKG Ltd	144	29 Sept	108303	Kelvin Ltd	160
					Salaries	9,024

Schedule of current standing orders

1. Monthly, on 16th of the month, £300.00 to West Council regarding rates.

2. Monthly, on 25th of month, £400.00 to Any Bank for hire purchase agreement.

J. Maclean

Chief Accountant

6 Reconciliations on a computerised system

In essence there is **no difference between reconciling a manual cash book and reconciling a computerised cash book**.

6.1 Computer controls over cash

In theory many of the same errors could occur in a computerised cash book as in a manual one. However, the computer will have **programme controls** built in to prevent or detect many of the errors.

Error	Programme control
Casting (addition)	Computers are programmed to add up correctly.
Updating from ledgers	When money is received from debtors, it will be posted to the sales ledger. The computer will then automatically update the bank account in the main ledger. This means that receipts and payments are unlikely to be confused.
Combined computer and manual cash books	The manual cash book reflects transactions generated by the computer system (for instance cheque payments from the purchase ledger), and also transactions initiated outside the computer system ('one-off' events such as the purchase of capital assets). The manual transactions will also be entered on to the computer. When a bank reconciliation is due to take place, the first job might be to make sure that the computer bank account and the cash book balances agree.

Key learning points

☑ A **bank reconciliation** is a comparison between the bank balance recorded in the books of a business and the balance appearing on the bank statement.

☑ The comparison may reveal **errors** or **omissions** in the records of the business, which should be corrected by appropriate adjustments in the cash book.

☑ Once the cash book has been corrected it should be possible to reconcile its balance with the bank statement balance by taking account of **timing differences**: payments made and cheques received which are recorded in the cash book but have not yet appeared on the bank statement.

Quick quiz

1   What are the three main reasons why a business's cash book balance might differ from the balance on a bank statement?

2   What is a bank reconciliation?

   A   Resolving a dispute between the bank and its customer
   B   Comparing the bank statement with the sales ledger
   C   Comparing the balance on the cash bank with the bank statement balance
   D   Comparing the cash book with the control accounts in the main ledger

3   What is a bank statement?

4   Cheque numbers are shown on the bank statement to aid _____. *Complete the blank.*

5   What are the two parts of a bank reconciliation statement?

6   Business bank accounts usually pay interest. True or false?

Answers to quick quiz

1   Reasons for disagreement are: errors; bank charges or interest; timing differences (for amounts to clear).

2   **C**. A bank reconciliation compares the balance of cash in the business's records to the balance held by the bank.

3   A bank statement is a document sent by a bank to its customers, itemising transactions over a certain period.

4   Cheque numbers are shown on the bank statement to aid **identification** (the amount only would not be enough).

5   (a) The adjustment of the cash book balance.
    (b) The reconciliation of the cash book balance to the bank statement.

6   False. Business bank accounts do not usually pay interest, but it depends on the individual business's arrangement with the bank.

chapter 9

Making
comparisons

Contents

1 Introduction

Management information helps managers plan, control and make decisions.

This chapter discusses how managers make comparisons between actual data and other data. In doing so they can assess the **significance** of the actual data for the period. Comparing current results with other data can make the information more useful. Comparisons may also help to show up any errors that have occurred.

2 Types of comparison

Many types of comparison are possible. The ones chosen depend on the needs of the individual and the organisation.

Common comparisons include the following.

2.1 Comparisons with previous periods

The most common comparison is when **one year's final figures** are **compared** with the **previous year's**. A business's financial accounts contain comparative figures for the previous year as well as the figures for the actual year. As company financial accounts are sent to shareholders, this comparison is obviously of great interest to them.

Some companies' financial accounts contain figures for the last five years. Comparing the figures for five years may be more valuable than comparing the figures for two years. **Long-term trends** become more apparent over five years. If the comparison is only over two years, one or other year might be unusual for various reasons. This will distort the comparison.

For management accounting purposes year-on-year comparisons are insufficient by themselves. Management will wish to pick up problems a lot sooner than the end of the financial year. Hence comparisons are often made for management accounting purposes **month-by-month** or **quarter-by-quarter** (three months-by-three months).

2.2 Comparisons with corresponding periods

Making comparisons month-by-month or quarter-by-quarter is most useful when you expect figures to be reasonably even over time. However demand for many products fluctuates **season-by-season**.

Example: Seasonal fluctuations

A company making Christmas decorations had sales for the quarter ended 31 December that were considerably greater than sales for the previous quarter ended 30 September. For the quarter ended the following 31 March its sales decreased significantly again. Should its managers be concerned?

Based on the information given, we cannot tell. All the information tells us is that most people buy Christmas decorations in the three months leading up to Christmas. Comparing the December quarter's sales with the quarters either side is not very useful, because we are not comparing like with like. People are far more likely to buy Christmas decorations in the December quarter.

A far more meaningful comparison would therefore be to compare the December quarter's sales with those of the December quarter of the previous year, since the demand conditions would be similar.

This example demonstrates where comparisons with corresponding periods can be very useful, in businesses where the trade is **seasonal**.

2.3 Comparisons with forecasts

Businesses make forecasts for a number of purposes. A very common type of forecast is a **cash flow forecast.**

Example: Cash flow forecast

GEORGE LIMITED: CASH FLOW FORECAST FOR FIRST QUARTER

	Jan £	Feb £	Mar £
Estimated cash receipts			
From credit customers	14,000	16,500	17,000
From cash sales	3,000	4,000	4,500
Proceeds on disposal of fixed assets	–	2,200	–
Total cash receipts	17,000	22,700	21,500
Estimated cash payments			
To suppliers of goods	8,000	7,800	10,500
To employees (wages)	3,000	3,500	3,500
Purchase of fixed assets	–	12,500	–
Rent and rates	–	–	1,000
Other overheads	1,200	1,200	1,200
Repayment of loan	2,500	–	–
	14,700	25,000	16,200
Net surplus/(deficit) for month	2,300	(2,300)	5,300
Opening cash balance	1,200	3,500	1,200
Closing cash balance	3,500	1,200	6,500

The purpose of making this forecast is for the business to be able to see how likely it is to have problems **maintaining** a **positive cash balance**. If the cash balance becomes negative, the business will have to obtain a loan or overdraft and have to pay interest costs.

At the end of the period, management will **compare** the **actual figures** with the **forecast figures** and try to assess why they differ.

Differences are likely to be a sign that some of the **assumptions** made when drawing up the original forecast were **incorrect**. Hence management, when making forecasts for future periods, may wish to change the assumptions that are made.

2.4 Comparison with budgets

Most organisations divide their long-term goals into:

- **Objectives** (measurable steps towards achieving their goals)
- **Action plans** (detailed steps for achieving their objectives)

The action plans are often expressed in money and provide:

- An overall view for management
- Assurance that different departments' plans co-ordinate with each other

The financial plan is usually called a **budget**.

A **budget** is an organisation's plan for a forthcoming period, expressed in monetary terms.

You can use budgets to check that the plan is working by **comparing** the **planned results** for the day, week, month or year to date **with** the **actual results**.

Budgets, like forecasts, represent a view of the future. However the two are not identical. Forecasts represent a prediction of what is **likely to happen**, the most likely scenario. Budgets may be a **target** rather than a prediction. The target may be a very stiff one and it may be far more likely that the business fails to reach the target. However management may feel that setting a stiff target may keep staff 'on their toes'.

Because comparison of actual data with budgeted data is a very important comparison for management purposes, we shall discuss this aspect in more detail later in this chapter.

2.5 Comparisons within organisations

Organisations may wish to compare the performance of departments and different sales regions.

Example: Analysis of results by sales area

PANDA LIMITED: ANALYSIS OF RESULTS BY SALES AREA

	Area 1 £'000	Area 2 £'000	Area 3 £'000	Total £'000
Sales (A)	600	500	150	1,250
Direct costs by areas:				
Cost of goods sold	320	250	60	630
Transport & outside warehousing	60	35	15	110
Regional office expenses	40	45	28	113
Salespeople's expenses	30	25	11	66
Other regional expenses	20	15	8	43
Total direct cost by areas (B)	470	370	122	962
Gross profit (A – B)	130	130	28	288

Alternatively comparisons may be on a product by product basis.

Example: Analysis of results by product

TEDDY LIMITED: ANALYSIS OF RESULTS BY PRODUCT

	Product A £'000	Product B £'000	Product C £'000	Total £'000
Sales	200	350	250	800
Variable costs of goods sold	95	175	90	360
Gross contribution	105	175	160	440
Variable marketing costs:				
Transport and warehousing	5	26	37	68
Office expenses	8	20	7	35
Sales salaries	15	44	25	84
Other expenses	2	7	6	15
Total variable marketing costs	30	97	75	202
Contribution	75	78	85	238

We shall discuss the importance of contribution in the next chapter.

2.6 Comparisons with other organisations

An obvious way of assessing how a business is performing in its chosen market is to **compare** its **results** and **financial position with** its **main competitors**. The main information that will generally be available will be the competitor's annual statutory financial accounts. Thus the comparisons are generally made on an annual basis.

For management purposes comparisons with competitors' positions (as shown in the accounts) will often give only a broad indication of performance. The information available in statutory accounts is limited. For example the accounts will not give a product by product breakdown of sales, something which would be of great interest to management.

2.7 Comparisons with ledgers

Suppose you receive a query from a customer saying that you have sent him a statement saying that he owes £5,000, when he believes he only owes £1,000. You check the balance on his account in the sales ledger and indeed it is £5,000.

However when you check the invoices that make up that balance, you see that two invoices totalling £4,000 were addressed to another customer, and have been posted to the wrong sales ledger account.

This example illustrates that you may need to compare the actual data on original documentation such as invoices with data in ledger accounts if **queries arise**.

2.8 Non-financial comparisons

As well as being made in **financial terms** (costs and revenues), you may make comparisons in other ways. For example you may compare units produced or sold. Other possible comparisons include measures of quality/customer satisfaction, time taken for various processes etc.

Example: A hospital casualty department

A hospital casualty department will aim to deal with incoming patients quickly, efficiently and effectively but numbers and types of patients are hard to predict. Comparing waiting times or cases dealt with per day will be misleading if one day includes the victims of a serious train crash and another covers only minor injuries. Long term comparisons might give a clearer picture and help to identify usage patterns (for example busy Saturday nights). Comparisons with other casualty departments might be even more revealing.

Activity 9.1

Do you think the comparisons given to the following individuals are the right ones to help them to assess the performance of their work teams?

(a)   Daily output in units compared with the same day, for the previous week, for a shift supervisor in a car factory

(b)   December sales value compared with the previous month for the sales manager of a firm trading in Christmas decorations

(c)   This year's examination results compared with last year for a secondary school headteacher

Tutorial note. Think about the relevance and completeness of the information.

3 Identifying differences

Differences are only meaningful if they **compare like with like.**

For example if the heating bill for the summer quarter is less than that for the winter quarter, the difference does not tell you anything about organisational performance, only about the weather.

3.1 Financial differences

If production quantities change from the amount planned or the amount produced in previous periods, then obviously costs will change but by how much?

The detailed techniques for dealing with this problem are beyond the scope of this Text. However in essence what you do is **adjust** the figures that you are comparing actual data with to take account of the changed quantities.

If production is 10% more than it was in the previous period, then we can expect the costs of materials used in the process to rise by about 10%. The effect on labour costs will depend on whether workers are paid a flat rate or by what they produce. Most factory overheads should not vary with the change in quantities produced.

3.2 Non-financial differences

Identifying differences only in financial terms may not be very helpful in finding out why they have actually occurred.

For example if raw material expenditure is greater than forecast, this could be due to a price increase or to using a greater amount than planned. In this situation **reporting quantities as well as prices** will be helpful.

Activity 9.2

Here is part of a sales budget for an ice cream manufacturer.

MONTH	Jan	Feb	Mar	Apr	May	June	Jul	Aug
000 Gallons	1.0	1.0	1.1	1.1	1.2	1.4	1.4	1.5
Sales price £ per gall	8.00	8.00	8.00	8.00	8.00	8.50	8.50	8.50

(a) The sales department complains that they only get information on quantities sold and would like to know what revenue they have earned. They ask you to compare budgeted sales revenue with actual for the last three months (April, May and June). Where would you find the actual sales figures?

(b) You find the figures which are April £9,000, May £10,200 and June £11,800. The sales department telephones you to say that the price rise planned for 1 June was actually brought forward to 1 May.

Produce the report the sales department has asked for and compose a note to go with it, commenting on the effect of the price rise.

4 Reporting differences

The main point of reporting differences from the budget is to help managers to take the appropriate action. This makes it vital that they can **understand** the reports they get, ie that the reports are:

- **Relevant to their responsibilities**
- **Not cluttered up with unnecessary detail**

4.1 Example of a report

Here is a production cost report for week 32 for the department making cartons. Output was 5,000 units, as planned. Changes from week 31 have been calculated. In both weeks, output was 5,000 units, as planned.

	Week 32	Week 31	Change
	£	£	£
Direct materials			
Cardboard	1,026	1,002	+24
Staples	498	499	1
Glue	251	249	+2
Ink	99	100	−1
Total direct materials	1,874	1,850	+ 24
Direct labour	825	810	+15
Total direct costs	2,699	2,660	+39
Factory overheads	826	840	14
TOTAL COST	3,525	3,500	+25

Some of these changes are very small and perhaps do not need to be shown in detail. An exception report could highlight the more significant changes on cardboard, direct labour and factory overheads.

Once you have identified important changes, you may need more detail to investigate them.

Activity 9.3

A ward sister in a private hospital has the following changes in ward costs reported as exceptional.

	Feb	Mar	Variance
	£	£	£
Nursing salaries	4,500	4,750	+250
Drugs and dressings	237	370	+133

(a) Which of these costs do you think the sister can control?

(b) She decides to investigate the drugs and dressings change and asks you to obtain information on budget, actual this year and actual last year. You obtain the following information from the management accounts and the budget preparation papers.

		Actual last year	Actual this year	Budget
		£	£	£
January	Drugs	175	182	180
	Dressings	62	72	70
February	Drugs	165	178	180
	Dressings	68	59	70
March	Drugs	170	300	180
	Dressings	60	70	70

Would you look any further and if so, why?

(c)   Do you think the drugs and dressings budget should be combined?

4.2 Example of comparison of non-financial information

Here is a report on the conveyancing department of a firm of solicitors for the year 20X1.

	Planned	Actual	Last year
Number of conveyances	300	290	295
Number of staff	3	3	2.5
£'000 Fees generated	155	156	145
£'000 Staff costs	62	65	56
£'000 Share of overheads	38	38	35
£'000 Departmental profit	55	53	54

This shows us that fees earned are well up on last year and better than planned, despite the fact that the number of conveyances are less than planned. Overheads are on target but staff costs are greater than expected.

Sometimes reports will include information in the form of **ratios or percentages** such as output per employee, profit as a percentage of revenue etc. In the example above, the number of conveyances per employee last year was 118, but this year it is only 96.7. Unless staff are doing more complex work, this needs investigation.

5 Comparing with budgets

We stated above that budgets can be used to check whether management's action plan is working. You compare the planned results for the day, week, month or year-to-date with actual results. Differences between actual figures and the budget are called **variances**.

5.1 Variance reporting

Variance reporting is the reporting of differences between budgeted and actual performance.

Variances can be:

*   **Favourable** if the business has more money as a result
*   **Adverse** if the business has less money as a result

Favourable variances are not always good for the organisation. For example failure to recruit necessary staff will result in a favourable variance (less wages). It may, however, mean that business does not reach its production targets.

Reporting variances to the appropriate person draws attention to areas which are not running according to plan.

Activity 9.4

Here is an extract from a monthly cost report for a residential care home.

	Budgeted	Actual
	£	£
Laundry	1,000	1,045
Heat and light	1,500	1,420
Catering	8,500	8,895
Nursing staff	7,000	6,400
Ancillary staff	10,600	10,950

(a) Calculate the variances for the above items in £ and % terms

$$\text{(Variance \%} = \frac{\text{Actual costs} - \text{Budgeted costs}}{\text{Budgeted costs}} \times 100\%\text{)}$$

(b) If company policy is to report only variances over £500, which would these be?

(c) If company policy is to report variances which are 5% or more of the budgeted amount, which would these be?

5.2 Responsibility accounting

Budgets are also used to allocate financial responsibility to individual managers.

For example, the training manager will be responsible for expenditure on training. These responsible people are called **budget holders** and will have to decide what action to take if costs are higher or revenues lower than forecast. Reporting to them is sometimes called **responsibility accounting**.

The budget process will often document the key results required from budget holders in terms of **quantity** and **quality** as well as money. These targets will clarify how managers at different levels in the hierarchy can contribute to organisational objectives.

	Key objectives
Chief executive	Profit of £5,000
	2% growth in market share
	Improve employee relations
Production manager	No increase in cost per unit
	5% increase in units produced
	10% reduction in factory labour turnover
Factory supervisor	Reduce wastage of materials by 5%
	Reduce machine downtime by 10%
	Initiate monthly quality meetings

This information helps managers to perform their function of **controlling** the organisation.

It is like a central heating thermostat with the budget as the temperature setting. Thermostats allow small variations around the setting but if the variation gets larger, they will take appropriate action (switch the boiler on or off) to control the temperature.

In the same way, many organisations only report variances over a certain amount to avoid overwhelming managers with unnecessary detail.

5.3 Exception reporting

Exception reporting is the reporting only of those variances which exceed a certain amount or %.

You can classify variances as:

- **Controllable**: can be rectified by managers
- **Non-controllable:** are due to external factors beyond managers' control

Budget holders may be required to explain why either type of variance has occurred and should take whatever action is needed. If the variance is controllable, management can take action to rectify problems. If the variance is non-controllable, management may wish to revise their plan. Either way budget holders are not necessarily to **blame** for the variance.

Example: Comparison with budget

A manufacturer of copper pipes has budgeted for expenditure of £25,000 on copper in month 6 but actual expenditure is £28,000. Possible reasons for this include:

(a)   **Price increase** by supplier. This may be controllable. The purchasing officer should try alternative suppliers.

(b)   **World price rise** for copper. This is non-controllable. The budget may need revising for the rest of the year.

(c)   **Higher factory rejection rate** of finished pipes. This is probably controllable but needs investigation. Is the raw material quality satisfactory? (if not, is this due to supplier, purchasing, warehousing?) Is the factory process at fault? (if so why? Poor supervision? Inadequate training? Machinery wearing out? – find out from the factory supervisors/managers).

You can see that reporting variances puts managers on the alert but only gives clues as to where the real problems lie.

Activity 9.5

A hospital decides to cut costs by reducing the number of cleaners employed by 10%. This results in a favourable variance in the budget reports. Is it good for the hospital?

Tutorial note. Think of any other impacts a drop in a number of cleaners might have.

The ways in which managers use budgets is a part of a continuous process of planning, monitoring performance and taking action on variances. This is sometimes called the **control cycle** and can be illustrated as follows.

5.4 The control cycle

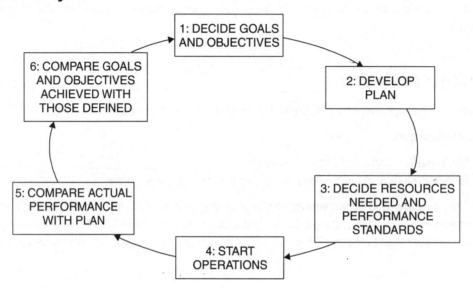

Activity 9.6

Here is an extract from a sales report for Region 3 in month 4 of the budget year (note that YTD stands for year to date, cumulative figures).

		£ actual	£ budgeted	£ actual YTD	£ budgeted YTD
Salesperson	Green	8,500	8,000	35,000	30,000
	Brown	7,600	8,000	25,000	30,000

(a)   What are the variances for each salesperson for month 4 and the YTD? Are they adverse or favourable?
(b)   Do you think they are controllable?
(c)   What action should the sales manager for Region 3 take?

Activity 9.7

A university librarian believes he exerts excellent management control because he has never overspent his budget and has tightened control over book stocks by reducing the loan period and increasing fines for overdue books. When applying for extra funds for a new book scanning system he is appalled to be told that library usage levels are far too low and that academic staff have resorted to keeping their own stocks of books and videos for loan to students. He suggests that these collections are immediately housed in the library, using staff from the information desk to catalogue and store them.

(a)   Are these suggestions sensible?
(b)   Is budget performance a good measure of library performance?
(c)   What other measures could you suggest?

5.5 Other uses of comparisons with budgets

Businesses obviously need to be **co-ordinated**. For example you cannot increase sales if you do not have the goods available, or increase stocks if you don't have the money to pay for them.

Variance reporting is important in alerting management to unplanned changes in one area of the business which may affect another. For example an unplanned decrease in production will affect future sales unless it can be made up.

In some businesses, comparisons with budgets are used as a basis for extra **rewards** to managers such as bonuses, or profit sharing. This makes the accuracy of forecasting and reporting very important to managers. It may lead to arguments over which costs are controllable by individual budget holders or the way in which fixed overheads are **apportioned** between budget holders.

Don't forget that **other comparisons** are often used in addition to budget comparisons to assess performance more broadly.

5.6 Format of comparisons of budgeted data with actual data

Your organisation is likely to set a prescribed format. An example is shown below.

Example: Management accounts

CARING CROAT LTD: MANAGEMENT ACCOUNTS FOR JUNE

	Month (a)	Budget (b)	YTD (c)	Budget for year Year (d)	Plan (e)
	£'000	£'000	£'000	£'000	£'000
Sales	95	100	1,000	2,400	2,800
Cost of sales	48	45	460	1,000	1,000
Gross profit	47	55	540	1,400	1,800
Sales overheads	18	18	175	430	500
Administrative overheads	11	12	101	245	260
Net profit	18	25	264	725	1,040

Purposes of each column.

(a) **Month**. These are the actual figures for the month of June.

(b) **Budget**. The budgeted figures for the month may have been seasonally adjusted or they may be just the total figure for the year, divided by twelve.

(c) **Year to date**. These are the actual figures for the year up to the end of June.

(d) **Budget for year**. This is the budgeted figure for the year. It is adjusted for the actual figures to date, to provide a revised target for the year.

(e) **Year plan**. This is the original budget for the year.

Activity 9.8

The information below shows budgeted and actual sales for the first six months of the year in money and in units. The sales manager gets a half-yearly bonus if his sales efforts are successful.

	Month	1	2	3	4	5	6	Total YTD
Budget	Units 000	9.1	10.0	10.2	10.5	10.8	11.2	61.8
	£'000	18.2	20.0	20.4	21.0	21.6	22.4	123.6
Actual	Units 000	9.0	9.9	10.2	10.3	10.6	10.8	60.8
	£'000	18.0	19.8	21.4	21.6	22.3	22.7	125.8

(a) What other department(s) in the business will be directly affected by the results shown?

(b) Should the sales manager receive his bonus?

Activity 9.9

You are the Accounts Assistant at Mark Balding's clothes factory (Mark Balding's Ltd).

As part of your month-end procedures, you have produced the following performance report for production cost centres for April 20X1.

PERFORMANCE REPORT		
	YEAR TO DATE 30.04.X1	
	Actual	**Budget**
	£	£
Materials	39,038	35,000
Labour	89,022	85,000
Expenses	18,781	15,000

Mark Balding is concerned that the year to date expenditure at the end of April 20X1 is not in line with expected expenditure and has asked you to report on any production cost variances which are more than 10% from budget.

Task

Produce a variance report with comments for Mark Balding.

Key learning points

☑ **Comparing actual results** with **other information** helps to put them in context and may show up errors.

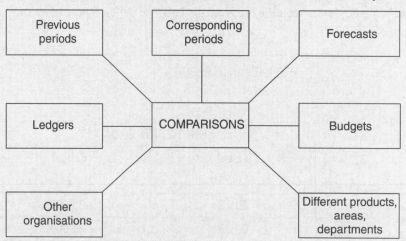

☑ Comparisons may be **financial** or **non-financial**.

☑ Choice of the comparison to make depends on the characteristics of the organisation, the individual and the activity being reported.

☑ When identifying differences you should ensure that you are **comparing like with like**.

☑ You should report differences in such a way that managers can understand them and pick out **vital information easily**. Comparisons should not be cluttered with irrelevant information or too much detail.

☑ Budget comparisons are popular because they show whether budget holders are account by the.

☑ **Variance reports** help budget holders to perform their function of control. The reports are especially useful if they separate controllable from non-controllable variances.

☑ Variance reports can also alert the organisation to factors which may **harm the planned co-ordination** of activities.

☑ An organisation may use budget reports to determine **extra rewards** for successful managers.

☑ Budget reports may be **combined with other information** such as non-financial information, ratios etc.

Quick quiz

1   Why are comparisons with forecast results useful?

2   What is an objective?

3   Why is a budget expressed in money?

4   What is an adverse variance?

5   Is it good or bad for the organisation?

6   Why is exception reporting popular?

7   Has a budget holder who does not overspend done a good job?

8   Why may managers be given non-financial as well as financial targets?

9   What is a favourable variance?

10 Why do some managers argue about the way in which overheads are shared out?

Answers to quick quiz

1   Comparisons with forecasts help to show if plans are being achieved and/or if the forecast was realistic.

2   An objective is a measurable step towards achieving organisational goals.

3   A budget is expressed in money to give top management an overall view and to ensure plans for different parts of the organisation co-ordinate with each other.

4   An adverse variance is a difference between planned and actual results which results in the organisation to have less money than forecast.

5   Whether it is good or bad depends on the reasons for the variance.

6   Exception reporting avoids information overload and makes it easier for managers to spot important variances.

7   Keeping within the budget is only one aspect of doing a good job. We would need to know whether other objectives had been achieved.

8   Non-financial targets are also important in achieving the organisation's goals and objectives.

9   A favourable variance is one which leaves the organisation with more money than planned, for example a cost lower than expected or revenue higher than expected.

10 Managers might argue because the method of apportioning costs may affect their bonuses, if their bonuses are based on the profits of their department.

chapter 10

Using management information for decision making

Contents

1 Introduction

Management information is used for lots of other purposes as well. You will cover some of these in your studies at Intermediate and Technician level, for example valuation of stock and assessment of risk.

This chapter provides an introduction to general **decision making**, to give you an idea of how management use the information that you provide.

We also discuss **pricing** which is one of the most important decisions management make. Set your prices too low, and you may not be able to cover costs. Set your prices too high and you may not be able to sell anything.

2 Making decisions

When providing management information for decision making, you must work out which costs and revenues are **relevant** to the decision. If in doubt, always clarify this with the person asking for the information.

2.1 Contribution

The manager of a factory making two products believes that one of them is much more profitable than the other and asks for a profit statement to compare them.

Profit statement			
	Product A	Product B	Total
	£'000	£'000	£'000
Sale revenue	100	120	220
Less: Direct (variable) costs	(40)	(70)	(110)
Less: Fixed production overheads	(20)	(20)	(40)
Gross profit	40	30	70
Less: Other fixed expenses	(20)	(40)	(60)
Net profit/(loss)	20	(10)	10

Do you think the company should stop making product B?

The important idea here is that products can **contribute** towards fixed costs provided their:

Sales revenue is greater than variable costs.

So for example if 1,000 units of a product are sold at £40 per unit and the actual cost of making those units is £25 per unit, then the excess of revenue over costs = 1,000 × (40 − 25) = £15,000. This £15,000 is available as a **contribution** to help pay for fixed costs such as insurance.

The idea of products contributing towards fixed costs is very useful for many decisions. It is an important concept within a system of marginal costing.

2.2 Marginal costing

Marginal costing is a system where only variable costs are charged as the cost of sale of an item. Fixed costs are charged to all products as an expense of the period.

In the example above a **marginal cost statement** would have made it clear that dropping Product B would decrease profits. The statement would look like this.

MARGINAL COST STATEMENT			
	Product A	Product B	Total
	£'000	£'000	£'000
Sale revenue	100	120	220
Less: Variable costs	(40)	(70)	(110)
Contribution to fixed costs	60	50	110
Fixed production costs			(40)
Other fixed costs			(60)
Net profit			10

In the example, Product B is making a £50,000 contribution to the total fixed costs of £100,000.

Activity 10.1

(a) Calculate net profit if Product B is dropped and no other action is taken.
(b) What other options could be considered?

Activity 10.2

Axle Ltd makes canned dog food for supermarkets to sell as 'own brand'. Each can costs 30p in direct materials and labour and sells for 40p. Axle Ltd's fixed costs for next year are estimated at £50,000.

(a) How much does each can contribute towards fixed costs?

(b) How many cans will Axle have to sell next year to cover fixed costs?

(c) If forecast sales are 750,000 cans, what will budgeted profit be?

(d) If these sales leave some spare production capacity in the factory, should Axle accept a special order for 20,000 cans at 35p per can?

2.3 Margin of safety

One way in which management use this information is to assess how safe the business is from making a loss.

Breakeven sales is the level of sales where:

Total contribution = Total fixed costs.

At this level the contribution from sales is just enough to cover fixed costs and the company makes neither a profit or a loss.

$$\text{Margin of safety} = \frac{\text{Budgeted sales} - \text{Breakeven sales}}{\text{Budgeted sales}} \times 100\%$$

$$\text{Margin of safety} = \frac{\text{Actual sales} - \text{Breakeven sales}}{\text{Actual sales}} \times 100\%$$

The calculation of the margin of safety provides a comparison between the sales needed to cover costs and the expected sales. In Activity 10.2 Axle Ltd's breakeven sales are where:

Total contribution = Fixed costs

Suppose X is the number of units sold needed to break even.

X (0.4 – 0.3) = 50,000

Therefore X = 500,000 units

As the margin of safety is a percentage, it can either be calculated using units sold or £ sales. Using units sold:

$$\text{Margin of safety} = \frac{750,000 - 500,000}{750,000} \times 100\% = 33.3\%$$

Put another way the safety volume of sales is 250,000 units. Axle Ltd will have to sell 250,000 less units before making a loss. The safety margin of 33.3% or 1/3 is quite large.

Activity 10.3

You are asked by the office manager to produce a report on the feasibility of your company installing a drinks vending machine in the office to sell coffee and tea at 30p per cup. At this price, she expects to sell 11,000 cups of tea and 17,000 cups of coffee. The information from the supplier tells you that you can purchase the machine for £2,600 or take a five year lease at £780 per year. An annual maintenance contract is available at £150 a year. The variable cost per cup is 22p for coffee and 20p for tea. Produce a report which includes an assessment of whether income will cover costs, whether purchase or leasing is the best option and any other issues you think are important.

Tutorial note. Remember to think about all the costs associated with the machine. What happens when the machine goes wrong?

3 Pricing

Pricing strategy depends upon two basic factors:

- **Cost**
- **Market conditions**

Obviously, in the long run the organisation must cover its costs or it will go out of business. Therefore the first step management must take when setting prices is to find out how much it costs to provide the goods or services. Management information systems should contain the necessary information.

Management must also take into account **market conditions.** The **degree** of **competition** in the market is an important influence. The demand for your product will probably decrease significantly if you increase its price, and make it more expensive than a similar product produced by your main competitor.

The **pattern of demand** must also be taken into account. As we have seen in the previous chapter, the demand for some products varies significantly month-by-month. So for example warm clothing can be priced at full price during the winter. However it is likely to be sold off cheaply during the warmer weather of the spring and summer.

The **strategy** of the business setting the price is another important influence on pricing. For example, a firm trying to enter a new market with well-established competitors will probably have to undercut their price to gain customers from the competition. However a firm with very little competition will have less pressure to drive prices down. For instance the only plumber within a twenty-mile radius will be able to charge high prices.

More can generally be sold at a lower price than at a higher one. However firms may not necessarily make the biggest profits by reducing prices. Firms may find it more profitable to have lower sales at a higher price, and therefore higher profit per unit. This will depend on how sensitive **market demand** is to price changes.

Management information for pricing must therefore include **external information** about demand, competition, market price etc as well as internal cost information.

Activity 10.4

Bottleo Ltd makes a corkscrew which sells for £5. Budgeted sales this year are 20,000 units at a variable cost of £2.20 and fixed cost per unit of £1.80. Management want to increase profits and have asked the sales manager to research the likely effects of changes in selling price. His forecast is:

Selling price per unit £	Sales volume (units)
4.00	29,000
4.50	25,000
5.00	20,000
5.50	17,000
6.00	15,000

He has added a note that if an extra £6,000 is spent on advertising, all these sales forecasts can be increased by 10%.

What would you advise management to do?

Tutorial note. Remember the importance of total contribution. How relevant are fixed costs?

Key learning points

☑ Management use **management information** to help them make a variety of business decisions.

☑ You will always need to know what information is relevant to the decision being made.

☑ **Marginal costing**, that is assessing the **contribution** which units sold make towards fixed cost, is one useful technique for assessing options for action.

☑ **Pricing decisions** depend on information about the market as well as cost information.

☑ Pricing decisions also depend on **company strategy**.

Quick quiz

1   If a firm reduced production its ………… costs will go down but its …………… costs will remain the same.

2   If a firm increases production the cost per unit will usually increase/decrease/stay the same.

3   A business will break even when total ………….. equals fixed costs.

4   What is the margin of safety?

5   Pricing decisions require information on costs and ……………………………………………

6   What will ultimately happen to a business if the selling price of its product is less than the cost of making it?

Answers to quick quiz

1   If a firm reduced production its **variable** costs will go down but its **fixed** costs will remain the same.

2   If a firm increases production the cost per unit will usually **decrease**.

3   A business will break even when total **contribution** equals fixed costs.

4   The margin of safety is the difference between break even point and forecast or actual sales.

5   Pricing decisions require information on costs and **market conditions**.

6   If selling price is below cost, eventually the business will become insolvent.

Answers to Activities

Answers to activities

Chapter 1

Answer 1.1

	Asset	Liability	Capital
Bank overdraft		✓	
Factory	✓		
Money paid into a business by the owner			✓
Bank account	✓		
Plant and machinery	✓		
Amounts due from customers	✓		
Amounts due to suppliers		✓	
Stock of goods for sale	✓		

Answer 1.2

Assets		=	Liabilities		+	Capital	
Goods	25,000		Owed to supplier	15,000		Capital	20,000
Cash (20,000 – 10,000)	10,000						
	35,000			15,000			20,000

Answer 1.3

Assets		=	Liabilities		+	Capital	
Goods	0		Owed to supplier	15,000		Capital	20,000
Cash (10,000 + 50,000– 5,000)	55,000					Profit (50,000 –25,000)	25,000
						Drawings	(5,000)
	55,000			15,000			40,000

Answer 1.4

Profit earned in the year	=	Increase in net assets	+	Drawings in current period	−	Capital introduced in the current period
35,000	=	50,000	+	5,000	−	20,000

Answer 1.5

(a) £60,000 (Purchases £75,000 – cash paid £15,000).
(b) £100,000 (Sales £150,000 – cash sales £50,000).

Answer 1.6

		Debit	Credit
(a)	Loan of £5,000 received from the bank	Cash	Bank loan
(b)	A payment of £800 cash for purchases	Purchases	Cash
(c)	The owner takes £50 cash to buy a birthday present for her husband	Drawings	Cash
(d)	The business sells goods costing £300 for £450 cash	Cash £450	Sales £450
(e)	The business sells goods costing £300 for £450 on credit	Debtors £450	Sales £450

Chapter 2

Answer 2.1

(a) Cash book
(b) Sales day book
(c) Purchase day book
(d) Cash book
(e) Sales returns day book
(f) Purchase returns day book
(g) Cash book

Answer 2.2

(a) The two sides of the transaction are:

    (i) Cash is increased (**debit** cash account).
    (ii) Sales increase by £600 (**credit** sales account).

CASH ACCOUNT

		£			£
07.04.X7	Sales a/c	600			

SALES ACCOUNT

					£
			07.04.X7	Cash a/c	600

(b) The two sides of the transaction are:

    (i) Cash is decreased (**credit** cash account).
    (ii) Rent expense increases by £4,500 (**debit** rent account).

CASH ACCOUNT

		£			£
			07.04.X7	Rent a/c	4,500

RENT ACCOUNT

		£			£
07.04.X7	Cash a/c	4,500			

(c)   The two sides of the transaction are:

(i)   Cash is decreased (**credit** cash account).

(ii) Purchases increase by £3,000 (**debit** purchases account).

CASH ACCOUNT

		£			£
			07.04.X7	Purchases a/c	3,000

PURCHASES ACCOUNT

		£		£
07.04.X7	Cash a/c	3,000		

(d)   The two sides of the transaction are:

(i)   Cash is decreased (**credit** cash account).

(ii) Assets – in this case, shelves – increase by £6,000 (**debit** shelves account).

CASH ACCOUNT

		£			£
			07.04.X7	Shelves a/c	6,000

SHELVES (ASSET) ACCOUNT

		£		£
07.04.X7	Cash a/c	6,000		

Tutorial note. As all four of these transactions relate to the same business, Joanne's cash account at the end of the day is as follows.

CASH ACCOUNT

		£			£
07.04.X7	Sales a/c	600	07.04.X7	Rent a/c	4,500
				Purchases a/c	3,000
				Shelves a/c	6,000

Answer 2.3

(a)	DEBIT	Machine (fixed asset)	£8,000	
	CREDIT	Creditors (A)		£8,000
(b)	DEBIT	Purchases	£500	
	CREDIT	Creditors (B)		£500
(c)	DEBIT	Debtors (C)	£1,200	
	CREDIT	Sales		£1,200

PROFESSIONAL EDUCATION

(d)	DEBIT	Creditors (D)	£300	
	CREDIT	Cash		£300
(e)	DEBIT	Cash	£180	
	CREDIT	Debtors (E)		£180
(f)	DEBIT	Wages expense	£4,000	
	CREDIT	Cash		£4,000
(g)	DEBIT	Rent expense	£700	
	CREDIT	Creditors (G)		£700
(h)	DEBIT	Creditors (G)	£700	
	CREDIT	Cash		£700
(i)	DEBIT	Insurance expense	£90	
	CREDIT	Cash		£90

Answer 2.4

		Original document	Book of prime entry	Accounts in main ledger to be posted to	
				Dr	Cr
(a)	Sale of goods on credit	Sales invoice	Sales day book	Debtors	Sales
(b)	Allowances to credit customers	Credit note	Sales returns day book	Sales/Returns inward	Debtors
(c)	Daily cash takings	Till rolls and/or sales invoices and receipts, bank paying-in book	Cash book	Cash	Sales

All these transactions would be entered into the double entry system by means of periodic postings from the books of prime entry to the main ledger.

Answer 2.5

				Memorandum	
	Account to be debited	Account to be credited	Dr	Cr	
(a)	Purchase ledger control	Bank	P. Jones	–	
(b)	Purchases	Purchase ledger control	–	Davis Wholesalers	
(c)	Purchase ledger control	Returns outwards	K. Williamson	–	
(d)	Fixtures	Bank	–	–	
(e)	Fixtures	Bank	–	–	
(f)	Purchases	Cash	–	–	
(g)	Sales ledger control	Sales	R. Newman	–	
(h)	Insurance	Bank	–	–	
(i)	Sales ledger control	Bank	J. Baxter	–	

Answer 2.6

(a)   *Purchase of goods on credit*

    (i)   The supplier's invoice would be the original document.

    (ii)   The original entry would be made in the purchase day book.

    (iii)   The entries made would be:

        DEBIT   Purchases

        CREDIT   Purchase ledger control account

(b)   *Allowances to credit customers on the return of faulty goods*

    (i)   The usual documentation is a credit note. Occasionally, however, a customer may himself issue a debit note.

    (ii)   The book of original entry would be the sales returns day book.

    (iii)   The double entry would be:

        DEBIT   Sales

        CREDIT   Sales ledger control account

(c)   *Petty cash reimbursement*

    (i)   The original documents would be receipts and a petty cash voucher.

    (ii)   The transaction would be entered in the petty cash book.

    (iii)   The double entry would be:

        DEBIT   Entertaining expenses

        CREDIT   Petty cash

Chapter 3

Answer 3.1

Tutorial note. You should be aware of the rounding rules when calculating VAT. This means that VAT is always rounded down to the nearest penny. So VAT of £15.979 is rounded down to £15.97

(a)

Customer	Zero-rated sales	Standard-rated sales (gross)	VAT
	£	£	£
1	72.06		
2		48.00	7.14
3 (1)		4.25	0.63
3 (2)	11.70		
4		−19.20	−2.85
5		92.50	13.77
6		100.00	14.89
7 (1)		58.80	8.75
7 (2)	42.97		
8		7.99	1.19
9 (1)		52.88	7.87
9 (2)	−8.40		
10		23.50	3.50
	118.33	368.72	54.89

The amount of VAT is £54.89. This is payable to HM Customs & Excise.

Total sales before VAT are 118.33 + (368.72 − 54.89) = £432.16.

(b)

		£	£
DEBIT	Cash account	487.05	
CREDIT	Sales account		432.16
	Value added tax account		54.89
		487.05	487.05

Tutorial note. You might have assumed the existence of a ledger analysed in greater detail. A fuller answer is shown below.

		£	£
DEBIT	Cash account	487.05	
CREDIT	Sales – books		126.73
	Sales – other		330.18
DEBIT	Sales returns – books	8.40	
	Sales returns – other	16.35	
CREDIT	VAT		54.89
		511.80	511.80

Answer 3.2

(a)   The relevant books of prime entry are the cash book, the sales day book and the purchase day book.

CASH BOOK (RECEIPTS)

Date	Narrative	Total £	Capital £	Sales £	Debtors £
June					
1	Capital	10,000	10,000		
13	Sales	310		310	
16	Waterhouses	1,200			1,200
24	Books & Co	350			350
		11,860	10,000	310	1,550

CASH BOOK (PAYMENTS)

Date	Narrative	Total £	Fixtures and fittings £	Creditors £	Rent £	Delivery expenses £	Drawings £	Wages £
June								
1	Warehouse Fittings Ltd	3,500	3,500					
19	Ransome House	820		820				
20	Rent	300			300			
21	Delivery expenses	75				75		
30	Drawings	270					270	
30	Wages	400						400
30	Big, White	450		450				
		5,815	3,500	1,270	300	75	270	400

SALES DAY BOOK

Date	Customer	Amount £
June		
4	Waterhouses	1,200
11	Books & Co	740
18	R S Jones	500
		2,440

PURCHASE DAY BOOK

Date	Supplier	Amount
		£
June		
2	Ransome House	820
9	Big, White	450
17	RUP Ltd	1,000
		2,270

(b) and (c)

The relevant ledger accounts are for cash, sales, purchases, creditors, debtors, capital, fixtures and fittings, rent, delivery expenses, drawings and wages.

CASH ACCOUNT

	£		£
June receipts	11,860	June payments	5,815
		Balance c/d	6,045
	11,860		11,860
Balance b/d	6,045		

SALES ACCOUNT

	£		£
		Cash	310
Balance c/d	2,750	SLCA	2,440
	2,750		2,750
		Balance b/d	2,750

PURCHASES ACCOUNT

	£		£
PLCA	2,270	Balance c/d	2,270
Balance b/d	2,270		

SALES LEDGER CONTROL ACCOUNT (SLCA)

	£		£
Sales	2,440	Cash	1,550
		Balance c/d	890
	2,440		2,440
Balance b/d	890		

PURCHASE LEDGER CONTROL ACCOUNT (PLCA)

	£		£
Cash	1,270	Purchases	2,270
Balance c/d	1,000		
	2,270		2,270
		Balance b/d	1,000

CAPITAL ACCOUNT

	£		£
Balance c/d	10,000	Cash	10,000
		Balance b/d	10,000

FIXTURES AND FITTINGS ACCOUNT

	£		£
Cash	3,500	Balance c/d	3,500
Balance b/d	3,500		

RENT ACCOUNT

	£		£
Cash	300	Balance c/d	300
Balance b/d	300		

DELIVERY EXPENSES ACCOUNT

	£		£
Cash	75	Balance c/d	75
Balance b/d	75		

DRAWINGS ACCOUNT

	£		£
Cash	270	Balance c/d	270
Balance b/d	270		

WAGES ACCOUNT

	£		£
Cash	400	Balance c/d	400
Balance b/d	400		

(d)   TRIAL BALANCE AS AT 30 JUNE 20X7

Account	Dr £	Cr £
Cash	6,045	
Sales		2,750
Purchases	2,270	
Debtors (SLCA)	890	
Creditors (PLCA)		1,000
Capital		10,000
Fixtures and fittings	3,500	
Rent	300	
Delivery expenses	75	
Drawings	270	
Wages	400	
	13,750	13,750

Answer 3.3

The main advantage of computerised accounting systems is that a large amount of data can be processed very quickly. A further advantage is that computerised systems are more accurate than manual systems.

Lou's comment that 'you never know what is going on in that funny box' might be better expressed as 'lack of audit trail'. If a mistake occurs somewhere in the system it is not always easy to identify where and how it happened.

Chapter 4

Answer 4.1

Customer	Credit limit			No credit
	High	Medium	Low	
Swansong	✓			
Helping Hands Agency			✓	
Bear and Stag Investments		✓		

These answers may surprise you! However other answers are possible.

Swansong is long established and has a good credit record, therefore it deserves a high credit limit. However if Joanne is cautious, she may start with a medium credit limit, to be reviewed after six months, say.

Helping Hands Agency is newly established and the owner has a poor payment record, therefore a low credit limit is appropriate. If Joanne feels that she is unlikely to be paid, she may decide to give no credit limit ie deal on a cash only basis.

Bear and Stag Investments is newly established. The chief adviser may be a City Analyst but has he the experience to run his own business? The credit rating is excellent, but the business has no past payment record and so Joanne should be cautious and start with a medium credit limit. This can be reviewed and increased later if needed.

Answer 4.2

Customer	Delete (Y/N)	Reason
Cash in advance	Y	These are not credit sales but cash sales.
Clears at end of month	N	A record is needed of the invoices issued during the month

Answer 4.3

(a)

CUSTOMER NAME:	Arturo Aski		ACCOUNT 001

ADDRESS: 94 Old Comedy Street, Vaudeville, 1BR, W. Meds

CREDIT LIMIT: £2,200

Date	Description	Transaction Ref	DR		CR		Balance	
			£	p	£	p	£	p
Brought forward 1/1/X7							2,050	37
1/1/X7	Inv	100	85	01			2,135	38
1/1/X7	Inv	102	16	99			2,152	37
1/1/X7	Inv	106	76	33			2,228	70

CUSTOMER NAME:	Maye West		ACCOUNT 030

ADDRESS: 1 Vamping Parade, Holywood, Beds, HW1

CREDIT LIMIT: £1,000

Date	Description	Transaction Ref	DR		CR		Balance	
			£	p	£	p	£	p
Brought forward 1/1/X7							69	33
1/1/X7	Inv	101	98	14			167	47

CUSTOMER NAME: Naguib Mahfouz

ACCOUNT
075

ADDRESS: 10 Palace Walk, London NE9

CREDIT LIMIT: £1,500

Date	Description	Transaction Ref	DR		CR		Balance	
			£	p	£	p	£	p
Brought forward 1/1/X7								
1/1/X7	Inv	104	123	10			123	10

CUSTOMER NAME: Josef Sveik

ACCOUNT
099

ADDRESS: 99 Balkan Row, Aldershot

CREDIT LIMIT: £700

Date	Description	Transaction Ref	DR		CR		Balance	
			£	p	£	p	£	p
Brought forward 1/1/X7							353	71
1/1/X7	Inv	105	35	72			389	43
1/1/X7	Cred	C44			353	71	35	72

CUSTOMER NAME: Grace Chang

ADDRESS: Red Dragon Street, Cardiff, Ca4

CREDIT LIMIT: £1,200

ACCOUNT 132

Date	Description	Transaction Ref	DR		CR		Balance	
			£	p	£	p	£	p
Brought forward 1/1/X7							1,175	80
1/1/X7	Inv	103	20	21			1,196	01

(b) Double entry

The sales ledger (ie the list of credit-related transactions analysed by customer) is a memorandum account.

So, the *double entry* from the sales day book and sales returns day book is as follows.

			£	£
(i)	DEBIT	Sales ledger control account	455.50	
	CREDIT	Sales		387.68
		VAT control account		67.82
			455.50	455.50
(ii)	DEBIT	Sales returns	301.03	
		VAT control account	52.68	
	CREDIT	Sales ledger control account		353.71
			353.71	353.71

(c) Additional items

(i) Did you check the sales return to the original invoice?

(ii) More importantly, did you notice that Arturo Aski (customer 001) has now exceeded his credit limit? How can this have slipped through the net?

　(1) The customer may have told the person who took the order that a cheque was 'in the post'.

　(2) The invoice might have been given the incorrect account code.

(3)   The person receiving the order might not have checked the customer's credit status.

(4)   The credit limit may have been raised, but you have not yet been told about it.

In any case, the matter should be referred to Ali for checking.

(iii)   Grace Chang has an outstanding balance of £1,196.01. When she next makes an order, the account must be checked to see that she has reduced the balance outstanding, as it is near her credit limit. In any case, you may wish to monitor the account to ensure that she is not having cashflow problems (and therefore represents a risk to you). If her business is expanding and she is settling debts promptly (which you will be able to ascertain by looking at the ledger history), it may be appropriate to review her credit limit.

Answer 4.4

(a)

CUSTOMER: RANJIT SINGH   ACCOUNT 1124
ADDRESS: 19 AMBER ROAD, ST MARY CRAY

Date	Transaction reference	Debit £ p	Credit £ p	Balance £ p
Brought forward				NIL
1/1/X7	236	405.33		405.33
2/2/X7	315	660.72		1,066.05
3/2/X7	317	13.90		1,079.95
5/2/X7	320	17.15		1,097.10
15/2/X7	Cash 004		1,066.05	31.05
21/2/X7	379	872.93		903.98
25/3/X7	Cash 006		500.00	403.98
31/3/X7	443	213.50		617.48
15/4/X7	Cash 007		500.00	117.48
1/5/X7	502	624.30		741.78
15/5/X7	Cash 031		500.00	241.78
	514	494.65		736.43
19/5/X7	521	923.91		1,660.34
20/5/X7	Cash 038		500.00	1,160.34
22/5/X7	538	110.00		1,270.34
20/6/X7	Cash 039		500.00	770.34
22/6/X7	Cash 042		923.91	(153.57)
1/7/X7	618	312.17		158.60
2/7/X7	619	560.73		719.33
8/7/X7	CRN 32		110.00	609.33
		5,209.29	4,599.96	609.33

(b)   From the sales ledger which you have reconstructed, it seems that Ranjit Singh owes you £609.33. How is this made up?

	£
Invoices raised	5,209.29
Specific payments	(1,989.96)
Payments on account	(2,500.00)
Credit note	(110.00)
Balance	609.33

Working back from the most recent items on the account:

(i)   Credit note number 32 for £110.00 can be matched against an invoice
(ii)   Cash receipt ref 042 for £923.91 can be matched against an invoice
(iii)   Invoice 619 for £560.73 is not settled
(iv)   Invoice 618 for £312.17 is only part settled.

This may look odd – invoice 618 being part settled when the only subsequent credit on the account (the credit note) relates to a different item – but it arises because the cash receipts on 20 June and 22 June led to the account being overpaid, ie it was in *credit*. This means that the excess credit was allocated against the next available debit, invoice 618.

You might have reached the same position by tracking *forward* through the account, eliminating 'matched' items and working through the payments on account, as follows.

Payments on account amounted to £2,500. This is deemed to cover the invoices as follows.

		£
Invoice	317	13.90
	320	17.15
	379	872.93
	443	213.50
	502	624.30
	514	494.65
	618 – part (ie balance)	263.57
		2,500.00

The balance remaining is:

	£
618 – unpaid part	48.60
619	560.73
	609.33

(**Note.** Invoice 618 is for £312.17, £263.57 paid and £48.60 unpaid.)

Answer 4.5

Account number	Customer name	Balance	Up to 30 days	Up to 60 days	Up to 90 days	Over 90 days
T004	Tricorn Ltd	94.80	0.00	0.00	0.00	94.80
V010	Volux Ltd	997.06	413.66	342.15	241.25	0.00
Y020	Yardsley Smith Ltd	341.77	321.17	20.60	0.00	0.00

Chapter 5

Answer 5.1

(a)   A creditor is a **liability** of a business. A creditor is owed money by a business.

(b)

Accounts	Purchase ledger (Y/N)
(i) Personal accounts for suppliers of subcomponents	Y
(ii) Inland Revenue	N
(iii) Customs & Excise for VAT	N
(iv) Suppliers of raw materials	Y
(v) Bank overdraft	N
(vi) Long-term bank loan	N
(vii) Telephone expenses	Y
(viii) Drawings	N
(ix) Proprietor's capital	N

Answer 5.2

(a)   The *Account name and address update* is used to set up some of the basic details of a supplier account on the computer system. It is also used to record changes eg change of address.

Updating can include both adding and deleting accounts. To tidy up the ledger, you can rid yourself of old 'dead' accounts.

(b)   Many transactions are posted to the purchase ledger accounts, for example:

(i)   invoices received from suppliers

(ii)   credit notes from suppliers

(iii)   payments to suppliers

(iv)   refunds of cash from suppliers (ie *Debit* Cash, *Credit* Creditors)

(v)   discounts received

(vi)   correction of mispostings

(vii)   allocation (in open item systems where monies paid are set against individual invoices, rather than simply used to reduce the balance)

Answer 5.3

(a)   By the open item method, cash paid is matched exactly to invoices.

So, the invoices for which no cash has been paid are:

		£
2/9/X7	P901	453.10
7/9/X7	P904	25.50
30/9/X7	P909	92.70
		571.30

(b)   By the balance forward method, cash paid is matched to the oldest invoices, so the outstanding balance is made up as follows.

		£
25/9/X7	P908	478.60
30/9/X7	P909	92.70
		571.30

Answer 5.4

ALFRED

	£		£
Returns	293.75	Invoice	1,175.00

BERTIE

	£		£
		Invoice	587.50

N GAS CO

	£		£
		Invoice	822.50

STANNER SUPPLIES

	£		£
		Invoice	705.00

PURCHASE LEDGER CONTROL A/C

	£		£
Returns DB	293.75	Purchase DB	3,290.00

VAT ACCOUNT

	£		£
Purchase DB	490.00	Returns DB	43.75

PURCHASES ACCOUNT

	£		£
Purchase DB	1,500.00	Returns DB	250.00

GAS ACCOUNT

	£		£
Purchase DB	700.00		

STATIONERY ACCOUNT

	£		£
Purchase DB	600.00		

BPP
PROFESSIONAL EDUCATION

Answer 5.5

A creditor's age analysis shows how long balances have been outstanding on the purchase ledger accounts. It may indicate that a business is delaying payment longer than is necessary or that it can not pay its liabilities.

Answer 5.6

- Purchase and purchase returns day books
- Purchase ledger balances by supplier
- Supplier statements
- Remittance advices
- VAT analysis
- Purchases analysis
- List of supplier accounts
- Mailing list of suppliers' names and addresses

Answer 5.7

Journal 28 August 20X7

		Debit £	Credit £
(a)	*Memorandum account adjustment (JNL 1)*		
	Purchase ledger – MPV Ltd	97.40	
	Purchase ledger – Kernels Ltd		97.40
	Being correction of misposting of invoice (Kernels' ref 21201)		
(b)	*Memorandum account adjustment (JNL 2)*		
	Purchase ledger – ASR Ltd	400.00	
	Purchase ledger – Kernels Ltd		400.00
	Being correction of misposting of 21/8 cash payment to ASR Ltd		
(c)	*Main ledger account journal (JNL 3)*		
	Purchase ledger control account (£42.84 × 2)	85.68	
	Purchases		85.68
	Being correction of misposting of Kernels Ltd credit note C91004		

	Debit £	Credit £
(d) *Main ledger account adjustment (JNL 4)*		
Purchase ledger control account	64.17	
Purchases		64.17

Being correction of double posting of invoice 20642

Memorandum account adjustment (JNL 5)

Purchase ledger – Kernels Ltd	85.68	
	64.17	

Being adjustment to reflect JNL 3 and JNL 4
(*Note*. As the memorandum account does not form part of the double entry, it does not necessarily have to balance.)

	Debit £	Credit £
(e) *Main ledger account adjustment (JNL 6)*		
Purchase ledger control account	37.50	
Sales ledger control account		37.50

Being double entry to reflect contra between Kernels Ltd's sales ledger and purchase ledger accounts.

Memorandum account adjustment (JNL 7)

Purchase ledger – Kernels Ltd	37.50	
Sales ledger – Kernels Ltd		37.50

Being adjustment to reflect JNL 6

KERNELS LIMITED

20X7			£	20X7			£
28/08	Misposted credit note	JNL5	85.68	27/08	Balance b/d		644.26
28/08	Misposted invoice	JNL5	64.17	28/08	Misposted invoice	JNL1	97.40
28/08	Contra	JNL7	37.50	28/08	Misposted cash	JNL2	400.00
28/08	Balance c/d		954.31				
			1,141.66				1,141.66
				28/08	Balance b/d		954.31

Chapter 6

Answer 6.1

SALES LEDGER CONTROL ACCOUNT

		£			£
Debit balances b/d	(1)	X	Credit balances b/d	(1)	X
Sales	(2)	X	Cash receipts	(3)	X
Bank (refunds)	(3) or (5)	X	Credit notes	(4)	X
Bank (dishonoured cheques)	(3) or (5)	X	Bad debt expense	(5)	X
Credit balances c/d	(6)	X	Discount allowed*	(3)	X
			Debit balances c/d	(6)	X
		X			X

Sources of entries

(1)   Brought down from previous period's control account once closed off.
(2)   Sales day book.
(3)   Cash book and petty cash book.
(4)   Sales returns day book.
(5)   Journal.
(6)   Calculated and reconciled with sales ledger total of balances.

Tutorial note

*   Discounts allowed reflects only cash or settlement discounts, not trade discounts.

**   Individual entries to the account would be dated and would have folio references to the appropriate book of prime entry/journal. These details have been omitted for the purposes of clarity.

Answer 6.2

ITEMS NOT APPEARING IN THE SALES LEDGER CONTROL ACCOUNT

1 and 2 Credit and debit balances on individual debtor accounts

Individual debtors accounts do not appear in the sales ledger control account, although the transactions which give rise to them (sales, cash receipts etc) do. The sales ledger control account is a total account.

3 Cash sales

The sales ledger control account deals with sales made on credit. Cash sales (*Debit* Cash; *Credit* Sales) have nothing to do with it.

5 Provision for bad and doubtful debts

This is a *separate account* from the sales ledger control account, even though it has the overall effect of reducing the value of the assets represented by the sales ledger control account.

7 Trade discounts received

These are discounts on what has been purchased, so have nothing to do with sales.

11 Credit notes received

These have the effect of reducing what *we* owe to other people, so they have nothing to do with the sales ledger control account.

ITEMS THAT DO APPEAR IN THE SALES LEDGER CONTROL ACCOUNT

4 Sales on credit

This should need no explaining.

6 Settlement discounts allowed

A settlement discount is given to a debtor who pays early, and so reduces the value of the debt. So if someone owes £100, but you say that you'll reduce the amount to £95 if they pay within 2 weeks, then they have received, and you have given, a settlement discount of £5. The whole of the original debt is cleared – of the £100 owed, your customer has paid £95, and you have basically written off £5 to the profit and loss account.

8 Cash receipts

These are payments from debtors. They reduce the debt.

9 Bad debts written off

Writing off a bad debt involves removing the debt from the sales ledger and making a corresponding entry to the sales ledger control account, and then the profit and loss account.

10 Sales returns

These arise when sold goods are returned and the return is accepted. The debtor no longer owes the money, so the debt is cancelled. Sales returns would be posted from the sales returns day book as a total, a method similar to the way in which total sales are posted from the sales day book.

12 Credit notes issued

A credit note can be issued to reduce the value of the debt. This might be the result of a sales return, or correction of an error. (Note that if separate records of sales returns are processed, credit notes would only be processed in respect of other items, so as to avoid any double counting.)

Answer 6.3

(a)

UNADJUSTED SALES LEDGER CONTROL ACCOUNT

	£		£
Balance b/d	12,404.86	Balance b/d	322.94
Sales	96,464.41	Returns inwards	1,142.92
Bank: cheques dishonoured	192.00	Bank	94,648.71
Balance c/d	337.75	Discounts allowed	3,311.47
		Balance c/d	9,972.98
	109,399.02		109,399.02
Balance b/d	9,972.98	Balance b/d	337.75

(b)

ADJUSTED SALES LEDGER CONTROL ACCOUNT

	£		£
Unadjusted balance b/d	9,972.98	Unadjusted balance b/d	337.75
Sales: receipts from cash sales		Bad debt written off	77.00
wrongly credited to debtors	3,440.00	Returns outwards: returns to	
Sales day book undercast	427.80	suppliers wrongly debited to	
Balance c/d	337.75	debtors	3,711.86
		Balance c/d	10,051.92
	14,178.53		14,178.53
Balance b/d	10,051.92	Balance b/d	337.75

Joanne has debtors of £10,051.92. She also has a creditor of £337.75.

Errors (v) and (vi) relate to entries in individual customer accounts in the sales ledger and have no effect on the control account in the main ledger.

Answer 6.4

(a)

SALES LEDGER CONTROL

		£			£
1.12.X6	Balance b/d	50,241	20X7	Returns inwards	41,226
20X7	Sales	472,185		Bad debts written off	1,914
	Cheques dishonoured	626		Discounts allowed	2,672
				Cheques received	429,811
			30.11	Balance c/d	47,429
		523,052			523,052

(b)   **Tutorial note**. Did you remember to check the casting of the list of balances?

		£	£
Balance per P Johnson			46,347
Add:	Whitchurch Ltd invoice, previously omitted from ledger	267	
	Rectofon Ltd balance, previously omitted from list	2,435	
	Casting error in list total (£46,747, not £46,347)	400	
			3,102
			49,449
Less:	Error on posting of Bury plc's credit note to ledger	20	
	P Fox & Son (Swindon) Ltd's balance included twice	2,000	
			2,020
Balance per sales ledger control account			47,429

Chapter 7

Answer 7.1

Answer C is correct.

Answer 7.2

(a) All of them.

    (i) Not all cash payments are to trade creditors, so a payment could be given a wrong main ledger account code.

    (ii) These could be found in a manual system, or could be caused by a fault in a computer program.

    (iii) Transposition errors could be caused if the purchase ledger, main ledger and purchase day book were separate, and there were manual postings.

(b) (i) Dividend payments and (iii) drawings do not relate in any way to trade creditors.

(c) FALSE. You might overpay a supplier, or pay before the goods have been received and invoiced, or pay the wrong supplier, or pay for goods subsequently returned and for which you receive a credit note.

Answer 7.3

FALSE

In any accounting system, whether computerised or manual, accounts can be altered by use of the journal. It would be quite possible to make adjustments to the purchase ledger control account which, for whatever reason, are not reflected in the purchase ledger. So, while the purchase ledger updates the purchase ledger control account, there might be other differences.

It depends on which type of accounting system is used.

Answer 7.4

JOANNE SMITH
RECONCILIATION OF PURCHASE LEDGER BALANCES WITH THE PURCHASE LEDGER CONTROL ACCOUNT AS AT 31 MAY 20X7

			£	£
(a)	Balances according to purchase ledger			54,842.40
	Add:	Account omitted	8,300.00	
		RNH's account undercast	620.40	
				8,920.40
				63,762.80
	Deduct:	Cheque not debited to SPL's account	5,000.00	
		Contra arrangement omitted	400.00	
				5,400.00
	Amended balance as at 31 May 20X7			58,362.80

Tutorial note. The cheque for £5,000 is deducted. If it had been properly debited in the first place it would have **reduced** SPL's balance.

			£	£
(b)	Balance according to the purchase ledger control account			57,997.34
	Add:	Discounts received entered twice	740.36	
		Purchase for April	7,449.60	
				8,189.96
				66,187.30
	Deduct:	Vehicle erroneously entered as purchases	6,400.00	
		Returns outward omitted from account	1,424.50	
				7,824.50
	Amended balance as at 31 May 20X7			58,362.80

Chapter 8

Activity 8.1

(a) **Sheet number 72**. The bank numbers each statement sheet issued for the account. Transactions from 1 March 20X7 onwards will be shown on statement number 73, and so on. Numbering the statements in this way allows the customer to check that none of its bank statements are missing.

(b) **Bank giro credit**. The bank giro credit system enables money to be paid in to any bank for the credit of a third party's account at another bank. Pronto Motors has paid in £162.40 for the credit of Gary Jones Trading's account at Southern Bank. A bank giro credit may take around two or three days for the banks to process.

(c) **£59.03 OD**. This shows that there is a debit balance (an overdraft) of £59.03 at the bank on 11 February 20X7. Gary Jones Trading is at that point a *debtor* of the bank; the bank is a *creditor* of Gary Jones Trading.

(d) **Direct debit**. Swingate Ltd must have authority (by means of a direct debit mandate signed on behalf of Gary Jones Trading Ltd) to take a direct debit from its account. This arrangement allows payments to be made to a third party without a cheque having to be sent.

(e) **Bank charges**. The bank may make various charges to cover its costs in providing bank services to the customer. The bank will be able to explain how its charges are calculated.

Answer 8.2

CASH BOOK

Receipts Date 20X7	Details	£	Payments Date 20X7	Details	£
	Balance b/d	596.74	21 Feb	Swingate	121.00
23 Feb	Bord & Sons	194.60	28 Feb	Bank charges	15.40
			28 Feb	Balance c/d	654.94
		791.34			791.34

Answer 8.3

JOANNE SMITH
BANK RECONCILIATION STATEMENT AS AT 28 FEBRUARY 20X7

	£	£
Balance per bank statement		611.93
Add outstanding lodgement (Warleys Ltd)		342.50
		954.43
Less: unpresented cheques		
800124	207.05	
800125	92.44	
		(299.49)
Balance per cash book		654.94

Answer 8.4

(a)   (i)   CASH BOOK

	£		£
Uncorrected balance b/d	24.13	Overdraft interest	24.88
Error in cash book	27.00	Balance c/d	26.25
	51.13		51.13

(ii)   GEMFIX ENGINEERING LIMITED
BANK RECONCILIATION STATEMENT AS AT 31 OCTOBER 20X7

	£
Balance as per bank statement (overdrawn)	(142.50)
Less unpresented cheques (total)	(121.25)
	(263.75)
Add cheque paid in, not yet credited on bank statement	290.00
Balance as per cash book	26.25

(b)   There are three reasons why bank reconciliation statements should be prepared regularly and on time.

(i)   The company's records should be updated for items such as bank charges and dishonoured cheques so that managers are not working with an incorrect figure for the bank balance.

(ii)   Errors should be identified and corrected as soon as possible, whether they are made by the company or by the bank.

(iii)   Checks should be made on the time delay between cheques being written and their presentation for payment, and to check the time taken for cheques and cash paid in to be credited to the account. A better understanding of such timing differences will help managers to improve their cash planning.

Answer 8.5

(a)

CASH BOOK

Date 20X0	Details	Bank £	Date 20X0	Cheque No	Details	Bank £
1 Sept	Balance b/f	13,400	1 Sept	108300	J Hibbert	1,200
1 Sept	L Peters	400	5 Sept	108301	Cleanglass	470
28 Sept	John Smith	2,400	25 Sept	108302	Denham Insurers	630
29 Sept	KKG Ltd	144	29 Sept	108303	Kelvin Ltd	160
8 Sept	Zebra Sales	4,000			Salaries	9,024
30 Sept	Bristol Ltd	2,000			West Council	300
					Any Bank	400
					Bank charges	132
					Balance c/d	10,028
		22,344				22,344
	Balance b/d	10,028				

(b)   BANK RECONCILIATION AT 30 SEPTEMBER 20X0

	£
Balance per bank statement	8,114
Less unpresented cheque 108302	(630)
	7,484
Add uncleared receipts (2,400 + 144)	2,544
Balance per cash book	10,028

Chapter 9

Answer 9.1

Tutorial note. In (a) the information is not precise enough, in (b) you are not comparing like with like and in (c) other comparisons are needed.

(a)   Daily figures will not help the supervisor to judge the performance of his particular shift (there are other shifts during the day).

(b)   You would expect December sales to be the highest for the year, so comparison with December last year and the year-to-date with last year might be more meaningful.

(c)   Exam results only measure one aspect of a school's objectives and will be affected by the quality of pupils as well as teachers.

Answer 9.2

Tutorial note. In (b) you need to quantify why the differences arose.

(a)   Actual sales revenue could be found in the ledger accounts for sales.

(b)   Sales Revenue Report April to June

	April		May		June		Total	
	Actual	Budgeted	Actual	Budgeted	Actual	Budgeted	Actual	Budgeted
	£'000	£'000	£'000	£'000	£'000	£'000	£'000	£'000
	9.0	8.8	10.2	9.6	11.8	11.9	31.0	30.3

Note

Sales revenue for the three months is £700 more than budgeted.

In April, the quantity sold was greater than budget resulting in £200 revenue over budget. In May, a price rise of 50p per gallon (not in the budget until June) resulted in an increase in revenue of £600 over budget although the amount sold was as planned. In June, the quantity sold was under budget resulting in a £100 revenue shortfall. This equates to the £700 increase above (£200 + £600 − £100)

Answer 9.3

Tutorial note. The key to this activity is determining who makes the decisions about which costs.

(a)   Nursing salaries would probably be centrally controlled by the hospital and influenced by NHS salaries. Drugs would be determined by a doctor and administered by a nurse. Dressings are probably the only item the ward sister has any control over.

(b)   The £300 drugs cost for March looks quite different from the normal pattern of cost. You should look at the ledger account and purchase documents to see if it is correct.

(c)   Combining drugs and dressings costs does not seem helpful in a ward report since only one is likely to be a controllable cost for the ward sister.

Answer 9.4

Tutorial note. Using % increase may result in small £ changes being highlighted (if budgeted cost is £1, actual cost is £3, the variance is 200%). However % variances may be a good guide to problems with the assumptions behind budgets.

(a)

	Budgeted	Actual	Variance	Variance
	£	£	£	%
Laundry	1,000	1,045	45(A)	4.5
Heat and light	1,500	1,420	80(F)	5.3
Catering	8,500	8,895	395(A)	4.6
Nursing staff	7,000	6,400	600(F)	8.6
Ancillary staff	10,600	10,950	350(A)	3.3

$$\text{Variance \%} = \frac{\text{Actual costs} - \text{Budgeted costs}}{\text{Budgeted costs}} \times 100\%$$

(b)   Only the cost of nursing staff

(c)   Heat and light and nursing staff

Answer 9.5

Tutorial note. This illustrates not only the importance of non-financial objectives, but also how failure to meet non-financial objectives may impact upon financial objectives.

This is only good if the necessary standards of cleanliness can be maintained. If they can be, then there were probably too many cleaners before. If standards fall, there will be other effects (like more patient infections) which will cost more in the long term and damage the chief goal of improving health.

Answer 9.6

Tutorial note. Note that the action to control the variance may be needed by Brown or the manager.

(a)

Variances	Month 4	YTD
Green	£500 (favourable)	£5,000 (favourable)
Brown	£400 (adverse)	£5,000 (adverse)

(b)   The variances may be controllable. The manager needs to find out why Brown is below target. If he has been sick or on holiday, he may need to make more calls in the next few months. However, he may need more training or greater incentives; if so the manager should try to provide what he needs.

(c)   The action taken depends on the reasons for both variances. Total sales for the regions are as planned for the year so far, so there is no effect on the production plan. The manager should assess whether Brown is really underperforming (see part (b)). Alternatively Brown may have more 'difficult' customers than Green. If so, the manager should consider changing targets or swapping some customers between the two salesmen.

Answer 9.7

Tutorial note. Another illustration of the importance of non-financial objectives.

(a)   The suggestions miss the point that the library does not seem to be meeting the needs of staff and students. Until this is remedied, there is no point (and probably no chance) of taking over staff stocks. Using information staff for cataloguing is not likely to improve library service either.

(b)   Library performance cannot be measured only in terms of money since low spending might mean that staff books, facilities etc are insufficient rather than that it is efficiently run.

(c)   Other measures should reflect the goals of the library service. These could include levels of usage (perhaps analysed by department), surveys of customer satisfaction, new books purchased, numbers of enquiries dealt with etc.

Answer 9.8

Tutorial note. In answering activities such as (a), you need to think about how what one department does can affect another. In (b) quantities sold might also be important as well as sales revenue. A decrease in quantity may imply that the business's share of the market has decreased.

(a)   The fact that sales are less in quantity than expected will affect the department which stores stock (there will be more!) and/or the production department (they may have to revise their plans and make less).

(b)   Although the quantity sold is below budget, the sales revenue is more than budget. Whether or not the sales manager receives his bonus will depend on how the company defines 'successful' for this purpose.

Answer 9.9

VARIANCE REPORT PRODUCTION COST CENTRES APRIL 20X1	
	Year to 30 April 20X1 £
Materials	4,038 (A)
Labour	4,022 (A)
Expenses	3,781 (A)

Comment

The significant variances which are more than 10% from budget are:

- Materials £4,038 (A) = 11.5%
- Expenses £3,781 (A) = 25.2%

Chapter 10

Answer 10.1

Tutorial note. In (a) the difference between the original net profit (£10,000) and the net loss if B is dropped (£40,000) is £50,000, the contribution of B.

B's contribution   = Sales revenue – Variable costs
                   = £120,000 – £70,000
                   = £50,000

In (b) note that there are a number of different options. The point in (iv) about the allocation of fixed costs is something we can only mention briefly here, but you will study the issues in depth at Intermediate level.

(a)   If Product B is dropped, its variable costs (£70,000) will be saved but the fixed costs will still have to be paid.

	Product A
	£'000
Sales revenue	100
Less: Direct costs	(40)
Less: Fixed production overheads	(40)
Gross profit	20
Less: Other fixed costs	(60)
Net loss	(40)

(b)   The company could

    (i)   Use the spare capacity freed by not producing Product B to make more of Product A

    (ii)   Investigate the possibility of using the spare capacity to make a new product

    (iii)   Raise the price of Product B

    (iv)   Investigate the way fixed costs have been shared between the two products

Answer 10.2

Tutorial note. (d) introduces the idea that there is more to pricing decisions than purely mathematical calculations.

(a)   Each can contributes 10p (40p – 30p) to fixed costs.

(b)   It must sell 500,000 cans to cover fixed costs (£50,000 divided by 10p).

(c)   Budgeted profit will be £25,000 = (750,000 × 10p) – £50,000 (fixed costs).

(d)   If there is spare capacity in the factory then this order will contribute an extra £1,000 to profits (20,000 cans × contribution of 5p). It might, however, upset regular customers if they got to hear of it.

Answer 10.3

Tutorial note. Note the following features about the report.

(a)   An introduction and terms of reference
(b)   Stating of assumptions (using the office manager's forecasts)
(c)   Report divided into clearly headed sections
(d)   Clear conclusions with a recommended course of action

The report considers the purchase cost issue separately from maintenance. Note that the costs of one option (purchasing outright and not taking out a maintenance contract) are uncertain; risk is therefore involved in the decision.

Cash flow may also be important. Even if immediate purchase is significantly cheaper ultimately than the other options, it will still be too expensive if you cannot come up with the money now!

The report might look something like this.

FEASIBILITY REPORT FOR OFFICE DRINKS VENDING MACHINE

Terms of reference

1   To determine whether forecast sales will cover costs
2   To compare the benefits of purchase or leasing
3   To identify any other issues which need consideration

Introduction

1   This report was requested by the office manager
2   I have used her forecasts of selling prices and sales
3   Other information comes from the supplier's literature
4   My cost comparisons are made over 5 years

1   **Will forecast sales cover costs?**

Both coffee and tea are to be sold at 30p per cup. Coffee costs 22p per cup and tea 20p per cup. Forecast sales are 17,000 cups of coffee and 11,000 cups of tea per year.

	Coffee	Tea	Total
	£	£	£
Revenue	5,100	3,300	8,400
Less Variable costs	3,740	2,200	5,940
Contribution per year	1,360	1,100	2,460

A 5-year lease on the machine would cost £780 a year which would easily be covered. The total lease cost over 5 years would be £3,900.

Purchase of the machine would be £2,600 and would be covered in just over one year

2   **Maintenance**

Under the leasing contract, maintenance would be undertaken by the supplier so the total cost of £3,900 over five years is not affected by maintenance costs.

Outright purchase could be combined with a maintenance contract at £150 a year. This would bring the total cost over five years to £3,350.

Alternatively, we could call in a repairer as necessary but, since the cost is unknown, this would be a more risky option.

3   **Cash flow considerations**

Outright purchase of the machine, although cheaper in total, requires a larger outlay at the outset. The leasing contract would spread the outlay more evenly over the five years.

Conclusions

1   On forecast sales, the costs of the machine are easily covered by whichever option is chosen.

2   Outright purchase without a maintenance contract is the cheapest but most risky option and puts the most pressure on immediate cash resources.

3   Adding the maintenance contract to purchase reduces the risk and is still cheaper than leasing.

4   The main benefit of leasing is to spread the cost evenly.

Recommendation

I recommend purchase of the machine and the annual maintenance contract.

Susan Scott

Answer 10.4

Tutorial note. Fixed costs need not be included in the calculations for pricing in this example. They remain the same whatever price is charged, that is they are not relevant to this decision. You will still get the same answer if you do include them, but it is quicker just to look at the contribution.

The price options will give the following results.

			Contribution	
Sales volume	Price per unit	Variable cost per unit	Per unit	Total
Units	£	£	£	£
29,000	4.00	2.20	1.80	52,200
25,000	4.50	2.20	2.30	57,500
20,000	5.00	2.20	2.80	56,000
17,000	5.50	2.20	3.30	56,100
15,000	6.00	2.20	3.80	57,000

A price of £4.50 will therefore give the highest profit.

If £6,000 is spent on advertising, then an extra 10% of sales can be achieved at this price.

This will only increase total contribution by 10% (£5,750) and is therefore not worth doing.

Glossary
of terms

There is a range of **documentation** that you may encounter in your studies and if you work in a financial environment. Some of the more common ones are listed with an explanation of their function

Advice Note

This is a document sent by the supplier of goods to the buyer to advise that the goods are being despatched.

Bank Statement

At regular intervals and in the case of a large organisation, daily, this document shows the bank balance on the organisation's account as seen by the bank. It rarely agrees with the organisation's own records therefore an exercise to reconcile the two balances may need to be performed to allow for timing differences.

Cheque

One of the most common methods of settling debts, this is a mandate allowing the debtor (who is owed money) to claim it from the creditor (who owes the money) by paying a cheque into a bank account, so that settlement of the debt can be completed by the banks own clearing system.

Consignment Note

When a third party haulier, not the seller, is making the delivery of the goods, a consignment note goes with the goods. The haulier has responsibility for the goods during transit. A representative of the buyer, often the storekeeper, normally signs a copy to confirm delivery and this is returned to the seller as proof of delivery.

Credit Note

A credit note is used to correct an invoice that may be wrong for a variety of reasons eg part delivery, overcharge, faulty or inappropriate goods.

Debit Note

This is sent by the buyer to request a credit note when the original invoice proves to be incorrect.

Delivery Note

This works in exactly the same way as the consignment note but is used when the seller is also making the delivery.

Enquiry

This is a request for information about the range of products, services and prices sent by a potential new customer before any firm orders are placed. It does not represent any agreement to enter into a contract between the parties; it is a request for information only.

Invoice

Sent by the seller it is a request for a debt to be settled at the appropriate time as agreed.

Order

If an enquiry has been successful an order will be placed which has contractual status.

Order Processing

Where a large order has been placed or the order could take some time to complete the buyer may send an order processing form to check on the status of the work and to confirm that delivery is still on schedule.

Statement

This works in a similar way to a bank statement but is sent by the debtor (who is owed money) to the creditor (who owes the money) showing the current state of the account. It is normally sent monthly showing the opening balance at the beginning of the month, transactions during the month and the closing balance at the month end.

**Stock/Stores
Record Card**

This is a manual system used by Stores showing which goods are available and in what quantities. It will also show the point at which more need to be ordered and the quantity of the re-order.

The following are supporting books and are not normally part of the double entry process, the exception being the Cash Book. They are often referred to as **books of prime or original entry** because they are the first point of entry of a document.

Cash Book

Where the cash and bank accounts are maintained in the Main Ledger the Cash Book itself will be a memorandum record only and used to record flows of money into and out of the organisation. However it is worth remembering that the Cash Book can also be a Ledger.

Journal

This book has three main functions. It can be used as a book of prime entry when others are not suitable for use to open new accounts. It can also be used to record unusual entries. This is more likely during the early life of an organisation. Once the organisation develops it is more likely to be used to make corrections or amendments to existing entries.

Instead of being used as some form of continuous book, vouchers may be used to initiate journal entries especially when there is much repetition of type of entry.

Purchase Daybook

Sometimes called the Purchase Journal, it is used to record all invoices received. Therefore it is an invoice listing. Where an organisation buys a range of goods the daybook may be analysed into categories of goods. In a computerised system the invoice listing fulfils the same function.

Purchase Returns Daybook

Sometimes called the Returns Outward Journal or Daybook it is used to record all credit notes received. Therefore it is a credit note listing. If the Purchase Daybook is analysed then so too will be the Returns Book. In a computerised system the credit note listing fulfils the same function.

Sales Daybook

Sometimes called the Sales Journal, this is used to record all invoices sent out. Therefore it is an invoice listing .Where an organisation sells a range of goods the daybook may be analysed into categories of goods. In a computerised system the invoice listing fulfil the same function.

Sales Returns Daybook

Sometimes called the Returns Inward Journal or Daybook, this is used to record all credit notes sent out. Therefore it is a credit note listing. If the Sales Daybook is analysed then so too will be the Returns Book. In a computerised system the credit note listing fulfils the same function.

Petty Cash Book

When an organisation deals primarily with cheques the main Cash Book will be used for them and a Petty Cash Book will be established to record and analyse those cash transactions that it perceives to be of petty (small) amounts.

The following records are those that can be part of the **double entry process** and thus provide the data needed to construct the Trial Balance and the final accounts of an organisation.

Cash Book

Used to record movements of money into and out of the business. There are many different ways of displaying this data from the one, two, three or four column presentation to those that contain records of cheques received and sent out only, cash transactions being recorded elsewhere.

Sometimes the Cash Book is a memorandum record only, (not part of the double entry system), cash and bank accounts being shown as part of the double entry process in the Main Ledger.

It is important when learning about the Cash Book to understand how it works and then to be familiar with different styles and layouts prior to testing.

Main Ledger

This has been known variously as the General Ledger and Nominal Ledger but AAT has indicated that it will be using the term Main Ledger in the future.

The Main Ledger contains three types of accounts. It contains all personal/private accounts eg drawings or capital. It also contains real accounts ie assets such as buildings, office equipment, etc., owned by the business. Finally the impersonal accounts themselves are included ie expenses such as rent, wages, control accounts etc.

In a computerised system the coding will usually reflect where the account balance will be found in the month end or year end accounts.

Purchase Ledger

Sometimes called the Bought Ledger this is a listing of creditors ie those to whom we owe money. It may be subdivided alphabetically, by region, buyer or type of creditor.

The Purchase Ledger may be part of the double entry system by taking the total of the balances from individual accounts and using that total in the Trial Balance for creditors.

It is more common today to use the Purchase Ledger as a memorandum record and refer to it as a Subsidiary Ledger. Total creditors would be obtained from a control account found in the Main Ledger.

Sales Ledger

This is a listing of debtors and can be subdivided in a similar way to the Purchase Ledger.

It is more common today to obtain the debtors total from a control account in the Main Ledger than to maintain the Sales Ledger as part of the double entry system. In this case the Sales Ledger would be referred to as a Subsidiary Ledger.

See overleaf for information on other
BPP products and how to order

AAT Order

To BPP Professional Education, Aldine Place, London W12 8AW
Tel: 020 8740 2211. Fax: 020 8740 1184
E-mail: Publishing@bpp.com Web:www.bpp.com

Mr/Mrs/Ms (Full name)
Daytime delivery address
Postcode
Daytime Tel
E-mail

	5/03 Texts	5/03 Kits	Special offer	8/03 Passcards	Tapes
FOUNDATION (£14.95 except as indicated)					
Units 1 & 2 Receipts and Payments	☐	☐		Foundation ☐ £6.95	☐ £10.00
Unit 3 Ledger Balances and Initial Trial Balance	☐				
Unit 4 Supplying Information for Mgmt Control	☐				
Unit 21 Working with Computers (£9.95) (6/03)	☐				
Unit 22/23 Healthy Workplace/Personal Effectiveness (£9.95)	☐				
Sage and Excel for Foundation (CD-ROM £9.95)	☐				
INTERMEDIATE (£9.95 except as indicated)			Foundation Sage Bookeeping and Excel Spreadsheets CD-ROM free if ordering all Foundation Text and Kits, including Units 21 and 22/23 ☐		
Unit 5 Financial Records and Accounts	☐	☐		☐ £5.95	☐ £10.00
Unit 6/7 Costs and Reports (Combined Text £14.95)	☐				
Unit 6 Costs and Revenues		☐		☐ £5.95	☐ £10.00
Unit 7 Reports and Returns		☐		☐ £5.95	
TECHNICIAN (£9.95 except as indicated)					
Unit 8/9 Managing Performance and Controlling Resources	☐	☐		☐ £5.95	☐ £10.00
Spreadsheets for Technician (CD-ROM)	☐		Spreadsheets for Technicians CD-ROM free if take Unit 8/9 Text and Kit ☐		
Unit 10 Core Managing Systems and People (£14.95)	☐	☐			
Unit 11 Option Financial Statements (A/c Practice)	☐	☐		☐ £5.95	☐ £10.00
Unit 12 Option Financial Statements (Central Govnmt)	☐	☐		☐ £5.95	
Unit 15 Option Cash Management and Credit Control	☐	☐		☐ £5.95	
Unit 17 Option Implementing Audit Procedures	☐	☐		☐ £5.95	
Unit 18 Option Business Tax (FA03)(8/03 Text & Kit)	☐	☐			
Unit 19 Option Personal Tax (FA 03)(8/03 Text & Kit)	☐	☐			
TECHNICIAN 2002 (£9.95)					
Unit 18 Option Business Tax FA02 (8/02 Text & Kit)	☐	☐			
Unit 19 Option Personal Tax FA02 (8/02 Text & Kit)	☐	☐			
SUBTOTAL	£	£	£	£	£

TOTAL FOR PRODUCTS £ ☐

POSTAGE & PACKING

Texts/Kits	First	Each extra	
UK	£3.00	£3.00	£
Europe*	£6.00	£4.00	£
Rest of world	£20.00	£10.00	£
Passcards			
UK	£2.00	£1.00	£
Europe*	£3.00	£2.00	£
Rest of world	£8.00	£8.00	£
Tapes			
UK	£2.00	£1.00	£
Europe*	£3.00	£2.00	£
Rest of world	£8.00	£8.00	£

TOTAL FOR POSTAGE & PACKING £
(Max £12 Texts/Kits/Passcards - deliveries in UK)

Grand Total (Cheques to *BPP Professional Education*)
I enclose a cheque for (incl. Postage) £ ☐
Or charge to Access/Visa/Switch
Card Number
Expiry date   Start Date
Issue Number (Switch Only)
Signature

We aim to deliver to all UK addresses inside 5 working days; a signature will be required. Orders to all EU addresses should be delivered within 6 working days. All other orders to overseas addresses should be delivered within 8 working days. * Europe includes the Republic of Ireland and the Channel Islands.

See overleaf for information on other
BPP products and how to order

AAT Order

To BPP Professional Education, Aldine Place, London W12 8AW
Tel: 020 8740 2211. Fax: 020 8740 1184
E-mail: Publishing@bpp.com Web:www.bpp.com

Mr/Mrs/Ms (Full name) _____

Daytime delivery address _____

Postcode _____

Daytime Tel _____

E-mail _____

OTHER MATERIAL FOR AAT STUDENTS	8/03 Texts	3/03 Text

FOUNDATION (£5.95)

Basic Mathematics ☐

INTERMEDIATE (£5.95)

Basic Bookkeeping (for students exempt from Foundation) ☐

FOR ALL STUDENTS (£5.95)

Building Your Portfolio (old standards) ☐

Building Your Portfolio (new standards) ☐   ☐

£ ☐   £ ☐

TOTAL FOR PRODUCTS   £ ☐

POSTAGE & PACKING

Texts/Kits

	First	Each extra	
UK	£3.00	£3.00	£ ☐
Europe*	£6.00	£4.00	£ ☐
Rest of world	£20.00	£10.00	£ ☐

Passcards

UK	£2.00	£1.00	£ ☐
Europe*	£3.00	£2.00	£ ☐
Rest of world	£8.00	£8.00	£ ☐

Tapes

UK	£2.00	£1.00	£ ☐
Europe*	£3.00	£2.00	£ ☐
Rest of world	£8.00	£8.00	£ ☐

TOTAL FOR POSTAGE & PACKING £ ☐

(Max £12 Texts/Kits/Passcards - deliveries in UK)

Grand Total (Cheques to *BPP Professional Education*)

I enclose a cheque for (incl. Postage) **£** ☐

Or charge to Access/Visa/Switch

Card Number ☐☐☐☐☐☐☐☐

Expiry date _____   Start Date _____

Issue Number (Switch Only) _____

Signature _____

We aim to deliver to all UK addresses inside 5 working days; a signature will be required. Orders to all EU addresses should be delivered within 6 working days. All other orders to overseas addresses should be delivered within 8 working days. * Europe includes the Republic of Ireland and the Channel Islands.

Review Form & Free Prize Draw – AAT Basic Bookkeeping (8/03)

All original review forms from the entire BPP range, completed with genuine comments, will be entered into one of two draws on 31 January 2004 and 31 July 2004. The names on the first four forms picked out on each occasion will be sent a cheque for £50.

Name: _____   Address: _____

_____

_____

How have you used this Interactive Text?
(Tick one box only)

☐ Home study (book only)

☐ On a course: college _____

☐ With 'correspondence' package

☐ Other _____

Why did you decide to purchase this Interactive Text? *(Tick one box only)*

☐ Have used BPP Texts in the past

☐ Recommendation by friend/colleague

☐ Recommendation by a lecturer at college

☐ Saw advertising

☐ Other _____

During the past six months do you recall seeing/receiving any of the following?
(Tick as many boxes as are relevant)

☐ Our advertisement in *Accounting Technician* magazine

☐ Our advertisement in *Pass*

☐ Our brochure with a letter through the post

Which (if any) aspects of our advertising do you find useful?
(Tick as many boxes as are relevant)

☐ Prices and publication dates of new editions

☐ Information on Interactive Text content

☐ Facility to order books off-the-page

☐ None of the above

Your ratings, comments and suggestions would be appreciated on the following areas

	Very useful	Useful	Not useful
Introduction	☐	☐	☐
Chapter contents lists	☐	☐	☐
Examples	☐	☐	☐
Activities and answers	☐	☐	☐
Key learning points	☐	☐	☐
Quick quizzes and answers	☐	☐	☐

	Excellent	Good	Adequate	Poor
Overall opinion of this Text	☐	☐	☐	☐

Do you intend to continue using BPP Interactive Texts/Assessment Kits?   ☐ Yes   ☐ No

Please note any further comments and suggestions/errors on the reverse of this page.

The BPP author of this edition can be e-mailed at: janiceross@bpp.com

Please return this form to: Janice Ross, BPP Professional Education, FREEPOST, London, W12 8BR

Review Form & Free Prize Draw (continued)

Please note any further comments and suggestions/errors below

Free Prize Draw Rules

1   Closing date for 31 January 2004 draw is 31 December 2003. Closing date for 31 July 2004 draw is 30 June 2004.

2   Restricted to entries with UK and Eire addresses only. BPP employees, their families and business associates are excluded.

3   No purchase necessary. Entry forms are available upon request from BPP Professional Education. No more than one entry per title, per person. Draw restricted to persons aged 16 and over.

4   Winners will be notified by post and receive their cheques not later than 6 weeks after the relevant draw date.

5   The decision of the promoter in all matters is final and binding. No correspondence will be entered into.